1001 little w...
spend less & li.. well

1001 little ways to spend less & live well

Esme Floyd

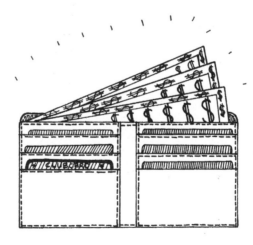

CARLTON
BOOKS

THIS IS A CARLTON BOOK

Text, design and illustrations
copyright © Carlton Books Limited 2009

This edition published by
Carlton Books Limited
20 Mortimer Street
London W1T 3JW

10 9 8 7 6 5 4 3 2 1

A CIP catalogue record for this book
is available from the British Library.

ISBN: 978-1-84732-350-7

Printed and bound in Dubai

Senior Executive Editor: Lisa Dyer
Managing Art Director: Lucy Coley
Design: Anna Pow
Production: Kate Pimm
Illustrations: Carol Morley

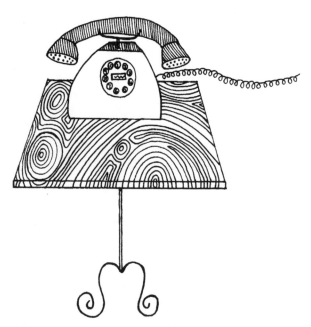

CONTENTS

INTRODUCTION

You might not be in debt, but you know your money isn't working as well as it could. Trouble is, how and where do you start to make things better? How do you save the pennies without turning into a penny-pincher?

This book is packed full of information for anyone who wants to get a handle on their finances and save a bit of money into the bargain. Covering everything from how to save on big financial decisions, like mortgages and insurance, to how to treat yourself for less and tips on how to get bargains in stores and online, this book is a veritable gold mine of money-saving miracles. With 1001 tips to choose from, covering all areas of life, there's something for everyone. Starting with just a few easy changes will set you on the path to financial freedom; simply choose the areas of your life you think need most improvement, pick your favourite tips and start making changes.

Top ten ways to spend less & live well

22
MONITOR SPENDING
(see Keeping finances in balance, page 12)

56
BE CHOOSY
(see Attitude to spending, page 19)

219
READ THE SMALL PRINT
(see Household bills, page 54)

281
BUY IN BULK
(see Shopping savings,
page 67)

473
SHOP AROUND
(see Building works, page 110)

501
DON'T ASK, DON'T GET
(see Fashion purchases, page 116)

698
GET A TOP TABLE
(see Dining and drinking,
page 155)

716
ADMIRE THE VIEW
(see Theatre, concerts
and cinema, page 159)

811
GO OFF-SEASON
(see Trips and holidays, page 178)

853
TASTE WINE FOR FREE
(See Cheap dates and
days out, page 187)

mortgages

1 SHOP AROUND

Don't trust your bank or building (savings and loan) society's mortgage advice – they will probably only advise you on their products. Instead, go to a broker who will be able to search a range of products to get you the best deal. Make sure you look at the exclusive deals offered by the big broker companies. Often, mortgage companies offer them great deals, that can be hard to match elsewhere.

2 FIND YOUR EXIT

Many mortgage deals will tie you in for an agreed amount of time, which means if you want to get out of the deal early you will be hit with a penalty fee. Be aware of how long you are tied in for and on what rate, and think about how your circumstances might differ over that period. Exit fees are similar – always check to see what fees you will be liable for if you want to change to another lender.

3 GENERATE SOME INTEREST

If you're a first-time buyer and a mortgage is too much to consider paying, why not go for an interest-only mortgage for the first few years to help save money? Remember, though, it's only a short-term plan and you should aim to overpay wherever possible to bring the loan down.

4 THE LOW-DOWN

Before you choose a specific mortgage, make sure you know exactly what you are getting yourself into. It's probably the biggest financial decision you'll ever make, so make sure you find out about how mortgages work before you take the plunge.

5 GET A RECOMMENDATION

With so many mortgage companies and brokers to choose from, finding the right one for you can be a daunting process. Ask friends and relatives who are in a similar financial position if they would recommend you, and make sure your broker knows it was a recommendation as sometimes they offer incentives.

6 KNOW YOUR PRODUCT

If you are using a mortgage broker, especially if they come on a recommendation, make sure you know which part of the market they are searching – some brokers limit themselves to a few products while others search across the market, which means they offer more choice.

7 BE ALERT

Even if your mortgage broker searches across the market, there are some lenders who never offer their products through brokers, so even if your broker gets you a great deal, spend a few hours checking through non-broker companies to see if they will match or better it.

8 DON'T BE FEE SHY

The best way to start a mortgage as you mean to go on is to find a broker that doesn't charge a fee, and relies on commission instead, leaving you in pocket. But do your sums – if there is a fee, but the deal is a good one that you can't find elsewhere, paying a fee might be the clever choice.

9 SEEK LOTS OF ADVICE

Most national mortgage brokers only charge you once you complete the mortgage, so there's nothing stopping you from approaching several for advice. But do make sure they aren't all doing credit searches, as that could actually make your credit rating worse and mean you don't get offered such a good deal.

10 BE SENSIBLE

Don't be seduced by 'money back' promises when it comes to commission and incentives. Make sure you look at the whole deal and unless you have a lot of money and mortgage knowledge, seek expert advice before signing up to a deal.

11 PLAN FOR COSTS

Some mortgage lenders will ask for all your fees up front, or on completion of the mortgage, and for some people these costs can be prohibitive. If this is the case for you, consider adding them to the cost of your loan to avoid short-term problems, but make sure you aren't paying more to do this.

12 BE FLEXIBLE

If you have a lot of uncertainty in your life, it might be worth your while going for a product with more flexibility. Some mortgages allow you to overpay, underpay or 'take a break', so think about what you need and try to find a mortgage to suit it. Ask your lender if you can suspend your mortgage payments without a penalty.

13 BE A CALCULATOR

When choosing a mortgage, you should always look at the percentage fees – some of the lowest rates of mortgage can have really high fees, around 2 or 3 per cent of the total loan, which could actually make a slightly higher rate more affordable.

14 DON'T BE DESPERATE

If you have had credit problems, minor or more serious, be wary of going to specialist 'bad credit' companies who advertise on TV and in magazines. The deals they offer are usually not as good as you can get elsewhere because they charge high fees. Most mortgage companies have a 'bad credit' section anyway.

15 DON'T BE SEDUCED

Some mortgages offer incentives like free valuation, low or nonexistent legal fees and free insurance. Don't let these freebies fool you as they are often worked into the total cost of the deal. Get your calculator out!

16 FIND A MATCH

To encourage people to go with them, and therefore secure a larger percentage of the market, lenders will sometimes offer 'match' rates, where they agree to match your interest rates, but also offer other incentives to reduce payments or fees. Always shop around to find these offers, which are not always available through brokers.

17 SAVE A DEPOSIT

One of the best ways to make sure you get a great mortgage deal is to save up a bigger deposit. Often, the best deals are reserved for those with a deposit of over 25 per cent of the value of their home, or in some cases 10 or 15 per cent. It is probably worth your while saving up for a while to make sure you have a reasonable deposit.

18 DON'T FORGET ASSOCIATES

While brokers are duty bound to offer you the best deals on national mortgage products, the same doesn't necessarily apply for associated products, so make sure you find out where they sit in the market and always get more than one opinion.

19 HOLD THE EXTRAS

Most mortgage lenders will also offer you a mortgage protection deal, but don't fall into the trap of automatically getting your insurance at the same place. Often, independent companies will offer you a far better deal, so shop around.

20 BUDGET, BUDGET, BUDGET

Before you undertake a mortgage it is really important to do a proper budget to work out how much you can really afford to pay. Remember that in addition you will have to pay local taxes, utility bills, insurances and household bills, so you need to take all these into account to make sure you never enter into a loan you can't comfortably pay.

keeping finances in balance

21 SET GOALS

Whatever your money-management goal is – early retirement, avoiding an overdraft or saving for a summer holiday (vacation) – make sure you keep it firmly in mind. It may also help to set small interim goals such as paying off your credit card within a set number of months or saving a certain amount in six months, then make sure you congratulate yourself every time you reach a goal.

22 MONITOR SPENDING

For a month (not December, when many people overspend, or February that's short) write down everything you spend. This means EVERYTHING! From stamps, parking and coffee to direct debits and credit card payments. Make sure that you write down every penny you spend then use it to see where you could make savings.

23 TAKE STOCK

Write a list of all your assets – include cash in your pocket, 'emergency' cash in the piggy bank in the cupboard, money in the bank and available balances from credit cards. Once you know what you have, it's much easier to work out how to use it for the best.

24 REMEMBER WHOSE MONEY IT IS

Even though credit cards, store charge cards and other lines of credit can be used to help you get what you want or need, remember that money in credit belongs to the creditor, not to you. So make sure you remember to calculate interest, finance charges and fees when you 'plan' for that money.

25 CONSIDER EVERYTHING

Remember that all of your possessions are potentially things you can turn into money, which could help you manage your finances better. You might not want to part with your plasma TV or car, but the ability to convert to cash is important when you're thinking about money balance.

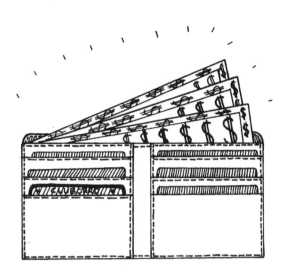

27 THINK LONG TERM

Remember, when you are thinking about planning your finances, long-term assets such as property and real estate, investments and personal property – like collections, artworks and antiques – usually appreciate in value over time and may help you to save money in the long run.

28 TRACK YOUR INCOME

Instead of working out your income on a 'paper basis' for money planning, make sure you take into account your real money, including things like sick days and overtime. Calculate what you really earn each month and try to build up a 4-6 month picture to base your calculations on.

26 CASH NOT CREDIT

Pay for everything you can with cash. If you find this difficult long-term, do it for one week to get a realistic idea of your outgoings. Don't use cheques, debit cards or credit cards as you won't be able to keep track of your actual spending. If necessary, put cash in envelopes labelled for different purposes and see if you can stick to that amount.

29 BREAK THE MONTHLY HABIT

If you are used to living hand to mouth, spending what you earn every month, breaking the habit might be hard but it will reap rewards in how you feel as well as your pocket. Stick to a plan to regain control of your finances and keep the goal in mind.

30 BE A DEBT MANAGER

Here's a surprising fact: you don't need to be in debt to be a good debt manager! In fact, thinking about personal debt management BEFORE you need it means you are more likely to get a good deal and be able to manage it better if you do end up needing to borrow.

31 MAKE A PLAN

The easiest way to lose control of your money is to let your lender make the decisions about your monthly payments. This is especially true for credit card debt, where lenders will often only take the minimum payment, meaning your debt doesn't reduce.

32 HAVE A PAY-OFF PLAN

Create a visual reminder of your debt that you can use to chart paying it off. A giant progress bar that starts with the amount you owe and ends with a zero, placed on your fridge or wall, will allow you to fill in the bar as you pay it off. It keeps your eye on the end goal – freedom from debt!

33 USE YOUR CREDIT

The best time to charge purchases to credit is when you really could pay cash. Although that's not always possible, it is possible to build a money reserve that can cover several months' expenses if you run into financial problems.

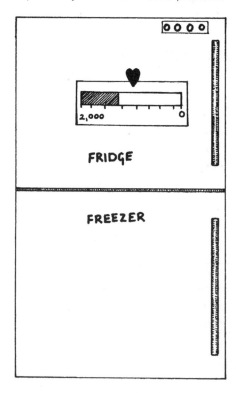

34 BE DISCERNING

Just because someone has written a book, an article or has a debt advice-related website doesn't mean they are an expert on personal debt management. Make sure you shop around and compare debt management advice. If several sources agree, it's probably good advice.

35 WRITE IT DOWN

In order to make sure you don't let your credit card run away with you, keep records of credit card purchases – what you bought, the date of your purchase and a plan of how you will pay it off. For instance, could you pay for that holiday (vacation) this month by doing overtime over the next three months to clear the debt?

36 PRIORITIZE DEBTS

Make sure you think sensibly about your debts when you are planning to pay things back. Pay off those with the most interest first, and get your calculator out to see how much you will really be paying so you can make sound financial decisions.

attitude to spending

37 SET A LIMIT

Ask yourself a question – how much money would you need to give you peace of mind or make you happy? Work out the answer and try to implement a plan to get you there within an acceptable timescale. Seek advice if possible.

38 BE HAPPY

Did you know that the richest people aren't the happiest? In fact, as society gets richer, people get less happy. Make savings part of your life, but make your life your priority.

39 LIFE PRIORITIES

Think about what your life priorities are: what do you want? Are those new purchases really important when you actually put them in the big picture? Try to spend your money on things that genuinely make your life better.

40 TAKE STOCK

Look around you at all the possessions you have (without regard to what anyone else has got) and the richness of your life as a whole. Start being grateful for what you have instead of reaching for the next thing.

41 SIMPLIFY YOUR LIFE

The simpler your life is, the easier it will be to keep a handle on your finances and live within your means. The more you spend, the more you have to work to earn, so pare back to just the essentials.

42 THINK QUALITY NOT QUANTITY

Choose to invest more love, time and expense in fewer things – one pet, one car, one house, even fewer children. Learn to appreciate what you have rather than always reaching for more.

43 CHECK YOUR BALANCE

Banks do make mistakes, so make sure you check your statements and balances regularly. They are usually quick to put errors right, but often it's up to you to spot them.

44 REMEMBER DELIVERY COSTS

Before you buy online or over the phone, make sure you take into account the delivery costs. Some companies will attract you in with low prices for items they then charge high delivery costs for, so make sure you compare the total price for your purchase to get to your door before you click to buy.

45 DO A COMPARISON

Always comparison-shop for expensive items. Subtract coupon and rebate offers from prices before you buy and check sale-priced items against the competition's regular-priced items to see if the offered discount really is a bargain.

46 EVEN IT OUT

Many people feel secure having savings, but if you have both debts and savings you are probably overspending on a large scale. The interest on your debts will almost always cost more than your savings are earning, so paying off your debts with your savings will leave you better off. Pay off expensive debts like credit cards and overdrafts first.

47 DON'T THROW IT AWAY

Remember the saying 'One man's trash is another man's treasure'? Before you get rid of things remember that throwing away something you could sell or swap is the equivalent to flushing money down the drain. Sell it on eBay or at a car-boot (garage) sale or swap it with a friend for something you need.

48 INCLUDE INTEREST

Tack on interest charges and credit card fees in addition to your principal payment on your credit card. For instance, if you plan to pay off your new television in five months, include the fees and interest from the credit card in the calculation so that you budget accurately to clear the debt in the time planned.

48 PAY IT OFF

Instead of simply paying the minimum payment, set a goal for paying major credit card debts – such as a payment for an electrical appliance – within a specific time frame, like three to six months. And don't let yourself consider buying another one until that is paid off.

49 STAY IN THE BLACK

On top of the embarrassment of having to deal with a cheque that has bounced or a card being rejected at the checkout, bank fees and overdraft arrangement fees can really cripple your finances. If you think you're going to go overdrawn, talk to your bank beforehand to avoid fees.

51 WATCH OUT FOR FEES

Most of the time, it will benefit your pocket to use cash instead of credit cards; that way you'll keep a better eye on savings and won't have to worry about interest payments. Be careful, however, of cashpoint machine (ATM) charges – make sure you only use machines that don't charge you for withdrawing cash.

52 THINK LOCAL

Discount stores can be great value, but take into account the time and expense of getting there before you shop around too much. Often, it's more economical to buy as much as you can from one place to avoid car-running costs and parking.

53 MAKE A LIST

Using a shopping list can eliminate return trips for forgotten items and also help you resist impulse buying. Crossing off items as you find them lets you know when it's time to go and pay and stops you falling foul of the supermarket's marketing strategies, like placing tempting foods next to the checkout.

54 PAY UP TODAY

Pay off small credit card purchases monthly. It might seem like you're being overcautious, but bear in mind that sale items or discount purchases are no longer bargains when interest accrues to the sale price. Even small debts can quickly grow out of control.

55 TAKE THE LONG VIEW

Just because you've blown your budget with silly purchases today, doesn't mean you can't start again tomorrow on the money-saving pathway. Commit to starting again and keep trying to get your budget accurate and refine your expenditure.

56 BE CHOOSY

Make decisions about what to buy BEFORE you get the sale coupons and discount vouchers out. If you wouldn't buy the item without a voucher or discount then you shouldn't consider buying it just because you can save money on the cost of it. This is what is know as a false economy – just think about how much you would have saved if you hadn't bought the item you didn't even know you even needed in the first place!

57 BE A SAVVY SHOPPER

Don't fall for 'no deposit' 'nothing to pay for years' deals in stores unless you are absolutely sure you will have enough money when the time comes to start paying for the item. If, for instance, you are on maternity or long-term illness leave, but will soon start to earn again, deferring payment for a year might be sensible. But, if you are likely to be in the same situation when you need to start making payments then it is unlikely that you will be able to find the money to pay it off.

understanding your habits

58 DON'T BE SAD

Research shows that if you go shopping after watching a sad film, you are likely to spend more. So make sure you only watch those tearjerkers when your money is tucked away somewhere safe!

59 DON'T DESPAIR

It's likely that at some point in your financial overhaul you'll hit a wall and feel despondent, but don't give up – try to keep the momentum going by reminding yourself of what you've achieved and talking to friends.

60 THINK PROGRESS

Change your expectations – there is no such thing for most of us as total financial security – but with work you can make progress towards it. Think of it as an ongoing process rather than a final destination.

61 SAVE YOURSELF

For many women, the fantasy of being 'saved' by a man from financial woes is still there, but times have changed. Make a deal with yourself to take control of your finances and choose a partner because they make your life happier, not because they pay off your debts.

62 UNDERSTAND YOUR EMOTIONS

If you want to save money, it's important to understand your emotional spending. Think about when you spend more money – is it when you're low or happy? Knowing when your danger times are will help you take action to change.

63 DON'T SPEND TO IMPRESS

Spending to impress your friends – whether it's giving lavish dinner parties, going 'one up' on home improvements or buying the latest fashions – is a common cause of overspending. Stop and think about what you are trying to gain by it, and talk to your friends to see if you can find other directions.

64 CARRY A PAGE TURNER

If you tend to shop in moments of boredom, why not find another way to release your emotions? Carry a romantic novel or thriller with you so that you can give yourself a fantasy fix. Or find another distraction, such as listening to your favourite music or going for a bracing walk.

65 KNOW YOUR WEAKNESSES

Everyone has different weaknesses – it could be eating out, window-shopping, eBay or online purchasing, mail-order catalogues or the latest fashion magazines. Identify your shopping weakness and cut it out of your life – for good.

66 GO STRAIGHT HOME

If you're having a bad day at work, don't allow yourself to go shopping on the way home. If you lack the willpower to do it yourself, call a partner or friend and ask for help. Get them to call you and tell you to go straight home, pick up only the essentials you need from the store or text a spend warning.

67 GET YOUR HIT

If you think you are in danger of blowing the budget because you desperately miss that shopping 'hit' and you can't get the same satisfaction from being in financial control, build a 'splurge fund' into your budget. Put away a set amount that you can use for whatever you want each month.

68 FIND YOUR FEELINGS

Talk with your friends about your spending feelings and try to identify which feelings are propelling you to spend money. Talking about it is a great way to raise awareness of all your spending habits and sharing feelings will help you feel less alone.

69 A SECOND INCOME

If you want to give yourself treats throughout the year but don't want to get into debt over it, why not think about getting a second income to cover all those extras? Do some overtime at work and put the earnings into a 'treat fund', or find that extra income from car-boot (garage) sales or selling items online.

70 THE BOREDOM FACTOR

Boredom is a major shopping trigger, so if you're online make sure that you set yourself a limit. Ask stores to hold things for you before you buy them (or save the page if you're online) and only buy them if you still want them when you go back a few hours later.

budgeting

71 PRIORITIZE EXPENSES

The very first thing you should do when you start your personal budget is to prioritize your expenses. Set them in order of importance and work down the list to see where you can make savings. There's no point doing a personal budget if you don't include money you would normally spend, so make sure you account for out-of-pocket expenses such as groceries, mailing costs and petrol (gasoline).

72 HAVE A CONTINGENCY

Even the strictest personal budget needs to take into account things that might happen unexpectedly. Try to build into your budget one-off costs like car or home repairs, so that when they do come they don't knock you off balance.

73 SEEK OUT RECEIPTS

For the last year, look at bank balances or receipts to see how much you have spent on unexpected costs such as dental bills or house repairs and try to create a monthly figure that would cover them. If you spend nothing on emergencies one month, carry it through to the next.

74 LOOK AT ANNUAL COSTS

When you're doing your budget make sure you remember to look at your bank balances for a year and include annual costs such as insurances, gym/club memberships and taxes, which you might forget if you look only at monthly costs. Divide these costs by 12 and include them in your monthly budget.

75 HOUSE AND HOME

Top priorities on any expense list are food and shelter. Shelter includes your rent or mortgage payment, local taxes and any home association or other housing expenses that may lead to the loss of your home. Along with discretionary expenses like fast food, magazines and other sundries, low-priority expenses include unsecured loans and credit card payments so don't enter into these arrangements.

76 CALCULATE YOUR INCOME

If you want to make a budget that works, you need to know exactly how much you earn. If you are paid weekly, calculate your monthly income by multiplying the amount you take home each week (after tax) by 13 and dividing by three.

77 DON'T BE ALARMED

When you begin personal budgeting it's not uncommon to find your expenses total more than your income. Don't panic – this is why you're doing it! Always take care of top priorities first, and then work on making practical decisions for the rest of your expenses.

78 DO IT MONTHLY

Make sure you don't just do one budget and then forget about it. Try to get into the habit of doing your budget for every month and practise sticking to it. That way you can account for monthly extras like people's birthdays, outings and entertaining and really keep on top of your finances every month.

79 GO GENERIC

When shaving money from your household expenses, consider purchasing generic items and store brands for a few weeks (or months) until your budget is under control. Then, when fees and bills are less, you can move back to your usual brands if you still want to.

80 PARTIAL PAYMENTS

Before you worry about how big your bills are, contact your utility companies and ask if they will take partial payments for a few months while you get your finances back on track. Most companies will be supportive if you contact them in good time and are pro-actively trying to manage your finances.

81 ROLL IT OVER

If an expense isn't a priority, roll it into next month's budget. However, if you can't pay a bill or meet a minimum payment, do contact your creditor and let them know when you will be able to pay. Don't let creditors make budget decisions for you.

working week

82 ONE-STOP SHOP

Many insurance companies offer good discounts if you take out more than one insurance policy with them. So, when it comes time to change your insurance, make sure you shop around for quotes that include moving your house, car and other insurances (such as life and medical) all together to one provider.

83 KEEP THE BALANCE

It might sound simple, but the absolute key to budgeting is spending less than you earn. If you really don't think you can reduce your spending, you'll have to find a way of earning more money or your finances will never be sorted out.

84 SAVE IT

If you're not managing to save regularly, try to budget money to put away in a savings account. Having a money reserve (savings) to fall back on in an emergency can make or break your budget. Even putting away a small amount each month is worthwhile and may come in useful one day.

85 CAR POOL

See if you can share driving costs if you have to take the car to work. Aim for every seat in your car to be filled and you should only have to do the journey one day a week. Or talk to your employer about whether they could provide some kind of economically efficient travel to work service. Often, they can get tax breaks on employee transportation, so it might pay them, as well as you, to investigate your options.

86 DRINK UP

If you don't get free tea and coffee at work, either take your own ready made in a Thermos or buy some tea bags or coffee granules and milk to make your own, rather than buying it. If your company doesn't supply free water, take your own in from home in large bottles to avoid spending money every day on small bottles, which are more expensive.

87 EAT IN

Going out for drinks with colleagues after work is a great way to wind down, but often means that you also end up eating out beforehand. If you know you're going out after work, take an extra meal into work with you so you can eat before you go out on the town.

88 BRING A PACKED LUNCH

The first thing to do to reduce work expenses is to make your own lunch. Buying sandwiches or lunch out is always more expensive and can often be less healthy, so try to get up five minutes earlier to make yourself a sandwich or salad.

89 BE MORE EFFICIENT

The best way to reduce the cost of commuting is to ask your employee about working from home. When you take into account the average time taken to commute to work, home workers save the equivalent of a staggering eight weeks of working days a year. Even working an extra hour a day from home would still make this pay for everyone.

90 THINK ABOUT CLEANING

When it comes to work clothes, reduce expenses by trying to choose items that don't need to be dry-cleaned, as this can increase expenses quickly. Instead, choose items that you can wash yourself.

91 ON YOUR BIKE

If you work close to home, a great way to save money on work expenses and even get healthier into the bargain is to get on your bike. Start with a few days a week and build up until you're cycling every day. You'll soon begin to enjoy your morning exercise and the spare change it leaves in your pocket.

92 GO PUBLIC

Whenever you can, choose public transport instead of driving your car. It is almost always cheaper to do this when you take into account fuel, running costs and parking. If you have to drive, choose a car that does as many miles to the gallon as possible.

93 TIREDNESS KILLS FINANCES

Spending money you don't need to when you're tired or hungry at the end of a working day or week is really common. Try to plan so that you spend at times when you are feeling alert, so shop in your lunch break rather than on the way home.

94 DO NOT VEND

Try to avoid buying anything out of vending machines, even if it is subsidized by your company, as it is usually more expensive. Instead, buy snacks and drinks from your usual stores and take them to work with you.

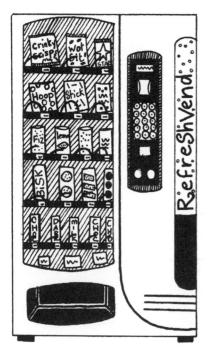

95 GET A THERMOS

If you commute to work, chances are you spend money on tea or coffee and even a little breakfast in the morning. But if you add these costs up, they can come to a staggering amount. Instead, buy a Thermos flask, drink your own coffee and save a small fortune every year. If you can't break the habit entirely, buy a coffee just once a week as a treat.

96 BUY IN BULK

Instead of buying the odd apple, orange or chocolate bar at work, go out at the beginning of the week and buy a bag of fruit or bag of treat-sized chocolates that will last you all week. It's a much cheaper option and will reduce the chance of you buying other snacks through the week as well.

97 TAKE CARE

If you're wearing your work clothes every day, it's worth investing in some key good-quality pieces that you can interchange. Make sure you look after your clothes and shoes, then you won't have to replaces them as often.

communication

98 DON'T MAX OUT

Be aware that the 'up to XMb' speed offered by broadband Internet suppliers is the maximum connection speed the provider offers. In reality the speeds you experience may be significantly lower, due to factors such as the quality and length of the actual line from the exchange to your home. Make sure you check the maximum you will get before you sign up to a higher speed.

99 FORGO THE LINE

Why pay taxes and fees on landline phone bills if you hardly use your home phone? In the USA 12% of adults aged 18 to 24 have abandoned landlines altogether. If you can, do without a home telephone line altogether and just use your mobile (cell) phone instead. Best for students and mobile professionals, you should consider the reliability of your mobile service and if your landline is essential for broadband or if there is another alternative.

100 GET A LINE

Watch out for bundles that include a home phone call plan, but no line rental. A jaw-droppingly low price may not look so appealing once you've added the telephone company's monthly line rental charge on top. Check the small print and go for the best overall deal.

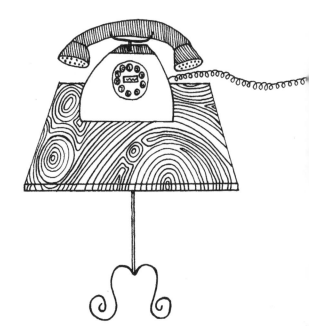

101 MAKE THE CALL

When it comes to phone bills, many companies now offer package deals that are far more efficient than standard deals. Look at your existing phone bill to see if deals, such as free evening and weekend calls, could help you to lower your bill. Choose carefully and opt for the one that's best for you.

102 WATCH YOUR WATCHING

Satellite and cable TV are great luxury options, but make sure you're not overpaying for your service – if you pay for premium channels, make sure you're using them and check back frequently with your provider to see if there is a more economical option.

103 DOWNLOADS UNLIMITED

If your broadband Internet package offers 'unlimited' downloads per month, make sure you read the small print on the supplier's fair usage policy to check there aren't hidden charges that might make your bills higher than expected.

104 THROW OPEN THE NET

If you want to make calls abroad, using your computer is much more cost efficient than using the phone and you can even make it a video-link call. Software like Skype or Siphone will save you money as all calls are free and it's usually free to sign up as well.

105 LIMIT YOUR PHONE CALLS

If you find it difficult to limit phone calls to friends and family, set a food timer for the time you think is reasonable – say 15 minutes. When the timer goes off, you know you must wind up the conversation.

106 BUNDLE IT UP

If you use broadband and a home phone, the chances are you could save money by taking both services as a 'bundle' from the same supplier. You can even take a 'triple play' deal that builds digital TV into the offering. Getting one bill is more convenient and service bundles could save you a significant amount each year.

107 GET THE RIGHT PACKAGE

When it comes to choosing a broadband package, make sure your usage doesn't go over your maximum allowance, as charges for doing so may be very high. Think about how much you will be downloading a month and ensure your new package will cover this.

108 PHONE AT NIGHT

Take advantage of your telephone company's offers on cheap calls – most of them offer savings or even free calls in the evening and at weekends, so try to call your friends or make your long calls at those times.

family finances

109 MOVING ON UP

Increase pocket money by a fixed amount on each birthday or on a set date once a year, such as the beginning of school. Let them be part of the discussion about how much they should get.

110 TALK IN THE FAMILY

Often children will ask lots of questions about money, like who is rich and who isn't. Explain to them that while some people struggle others don't have to worry about money, but they may have other struggles. Also explain that money matters are private.

111 SEE IT GROW

There are lots of kids' piggy banks available, but the best kind are the transparent ones that let your kids see their money grow, or use a plain glass jar if you can't find a novelty bank. Encourage your child to save change after a day of shopping, pocket money or coins from the tooth fairy.

When the piggy bank is full, help your child count and sort the money and decide what to do with it.

112 WORK OR STAY

If you're on maternity leave, make sure you do the full sums before you start going back to work – on the one hand there's your income, on the other, childcare and travel costs as well as subsistence (work lunches often cost more, for example). Make sure you really understand what your best financial option is.

113 KEEP MONEY SAFE

Provide your child with a place to keep his or her money. A couple of good money carriers for kids are money belts and neck pouches, to help prevent the loss of a wallet or purse while shopping. If they want you to carry it don't refuse, but encourage them to be independent.

114 TAKE THE LONG VIEW

If your children go on to higher education, you're likely to need substantial funds to help support them. Try to plan to finish paying your mortgage at the time they are due to start so you'll have extra income to help cover the costs.

115 MAKE THEM EARN IT

You will probably give your children an allowance, but there's no need to give it to them for free. Cover their basic allowance necessities with a small amount and give them the chance to do chores to earn extra.

116 SPLIT THE DIFFERENCE

If your child wants something expensive, you can teach them a good lesson about savings and value. Why not be honest and tell them it's too expensive, but if they save half the money you'll match it. They'll either do it or opt for something cheaper, but either way you've taught them a great lesson about money.

117 START AN ACCOUNT

As early as you can, start a savings account for your child and encourage them to be in control of their finances – visit the bank with them to deposit money and let them see their money grow.

118 START EARLY

When it comes to teaching kids about money, games like Payday and Monopoly Junior are fun tools – play with them and encourage them to ask questions. Start helping your child to learn to manage money the first time he or she gets some and is old enough to understand. For instance, when they receive a monetary birthday gift help them choose sensibly what to do with it.

119 GO COMPARE

It might be many parents' idea of hell, but going to the supermarket with your children is a great way to teach them about value and money. Help them compare prices and let them share the decision making about, for example, which brand of cereal to buy.

120 PLAN WELL

The key to being able to help and enjoy your family through the years is good financial planning. Planning for a pension when you have young children, for example, is a good way to make sure you're able to enjoy possible grandchildren in the future.

121 PLAY SHOPPING

Help explain to your child how money works by playing shopping – there are usually inexpensive checkout games hanging around in charity and second-hand stores, or make your own using piles of pennies and some vegetables and cans from your kitchen.

122 BE FAIR

If one of your children is better at saving, work with the other to help them save better rather than giving in and giving them extra. Otherwise you're sending the message that the saving child doesn't get as much, and children have a strong sense of fairness.

123 GIVE THEM CONTROL

Remember your children's money belongs to your children. Be supportive and advise and encourage them to spend and save wisely, but allow your children to make their own money-management decisions and pay the resulting consequences or reap the rewards.

124 GROUP UP

One of the best ways to save money as a parent is to form a baby-sitting group where you give each other hours of baby-sitting. Either do it informally or work out a token system whereby you all do the same amount, and then you can enjoy your free evenings out!

125 JOIN THE CLUB

Supermarket baby and kids clubs often have great vouchers and offers. It's usually free to sign up so it's worth doing, especially if you can be flexible about brands – offers on food and nappies (diapers) will often switch brands every few months and if you can move with them, you'll save.

126 THINK AHEAD

If you had an accident or became disabled or ill for a long time, would your family be able to manage? If not, think about buying accident or sickness cover so that you'd have a guaranteed income in the event of being unable to work. This is especially important if you're self-employed, but even if you're employed check your contract terms.

127 MAKE A WILL

Not making a will could quite literally be like throwing your money out of the window. Make sure – especially if you have children – that you've thought about where your money will go if something happens to you and how they'll be looked after.

128 SWAP IT

Get some mum friends together at your home and instruct everyone to bring five items for swapping – kids' clothing, a cookbook, magazines, unwanted DVDs/CDs, toys, etc. Everyone must bring exactly five items/bundles in order for this to work, and you could set a rough value.

129 GET COVERED

Nobody wants to think about dying, but taking out life cover is a good way to ensure that your family will be provided for if the worst thing happens. In some countries you will need to make sure the policy is written in trust, so the proceeds aren't taxed as part of your estate when you die.

130 GO FOR QUALITY

Buy as cheap as you can, but keep an eye on false economies. Buying that cheap brand of nappy (diaper) is only a saving if you don't have to use loads more because they leak or lack absorbency.

131 FAMILY TREATS

Children love treats and they don't have to be expensive. Think about cheap options, such as going to the park or on a nature walk, eating ice cream on the beach or simply asking them to choose what to have for breakfast or dinner. Even little changes to the daily routine, such as making popcorn and renting a DVD, can feel like a treat.

single-income households

132 BUILD A SPREADSHEET

Learn how to work with a spreadsheet on the computer (or draw one up by hand if you don't have a computer) so you can track spending and saving over the weeks and months – it will give you a great sense of control over your finances.

133 THINK ESSENTIAL

If you're on your own, or only one of you is earning, it's even more important to understand the difference between essentials and luxuries. Make lists of what you need as opposed to want, and try to make the latter as small as possible.

134 LOOK FOR A REASON

Whenever you get your money out ask yourself if there three reasons you need the item. Learning to question before you buy is a great way to change your money habits.

135 BE A GOOD BOOKKEEPER

Get into the habit of balancing your books every day, taking into account everything you spend. If you do it regularly it won't take long so try and incorporate it into your daily routine – before you sit down to dinner, for instance, or after the kids are in bed.

136 BANK BIG PAYMENTS

If you get a big payment during the year, such as a gift, tax refund or even some increases in benefits, the sensible thing to do is pay off debts. However, if you're in a single-income household it might actually pay you to bank this for use as an emergency fund through the year.

137 GET A MONEY BUDDY

One of the disadvantages of being on your own is you have to make all the decisions. Get a money buddy to help you decide when spending is essential – you could even give them some control over your petty savings. Or join a money club, which works on the same idea.

138 ADD YOUR INTEREST

If you're trying to balance your books, make sure you take into account all your credit card and other interest-charging debts and loans (apart from mortgages). Try to build in paying off the interest into your minimum spend so you're not racking up costs.

student households

139 GIVE YOURSELF AN ALLOWANCE

If you're relying on funds and loans that comes through in one lump sum, you'll need to carefully work out how to make the money last until the next payment. Calculate how many weeks you need it to last and give yourself a weekly spending limit. Doing it weekly is a good idea because if you overspend you only have to wait a few days until the next allowance comes through when you can correct it.

140 BANK IT

Why not create an emergency fund in a piggy bank so you know you've always got some spare cash for emergency purchases if you go over budget? Put spare change into it and compile a list of acceptable 'emergencies' so you don't splurge it on unnecessary extras.

141 BUY USED BOOKS

Wherever you can, try to buy used books from campus stores, local bookstores, Internet sites like eBay and from the ads on campus, in the library and in local stores. Try to share book expenses with friends or use the library where you can, especially for books you aren't likely to refer to again and again.

142 KEEP A DIARY

Make sure you keep a diary of all the closing dates for applications for things like grants, loans and scholarships. Missing a deadline is a sure-fire way to make sure your application is turned down, so keep those dates uppermost in your mind.

143 BENEFIT FROM YOUR INTERESTS

Join university clubs and societies that subsidize leisure and social activities. For example, being on a sports team could gain you access to a stadium event at a cut-down price, or belonging to the French club could get you free tickets to foreign films.

144 GET COMPUTER CLEVER

If you're buying a computer, save by shopping with student specials – discounts, rebates and back-to-school specials. Do your research for the best savings.

145 TALK ABOUT IT

Score big savings on student expenses by talking to other students – sharing information about discounts is a great way to get in the know about possible savings without doing days of research. Talking to roommates means you can start combining purchases to make bulk savings.

146 ASK FOR A DISCOUNT

Going to the cinema, buying music or getting into gigs, taking a bus, purchasing clothes, eating in a restaurant or even ordering pizza might cost less if you show your student identification card. Check local stores as well as travel companies for student discounts. In fact, wherever you go ask if there's a student discount, and you might be surprised how much money you can save.

147 CUT YOUR CARDS

To avoid getting into debt, have only one major credit card and use it sparingly. Set your own credit limit that you know you can comfortably repay. Just because the credit card company offer you a limit, doesn't mean you have to use it. Cut up all your other credit cards so you won't be tempted to spend on them.

health & fitness

148 GO TO SCHOOL

If you live near a school, find out if they run schemes in school holidays where you could use the facilities. Many schools let local residents use their facilities for a nominal fee, so check yours out and get moving.

149 FIND A RUNNING BUDDY

Running is one of the best ways to stay fit for free, but it's easy to back out if it's only you running. Find a running buddy to go with who is of a similar standard to you and you can help motivate each other to keep going.

150 TRY IT OUT

Before joining any gym it's always worth trying it out for atmosphere and facilities. Luckily, many offer free trials for a day or weekend, or sometimes there are web vouchers allowing you a longer trial. Ask your friends to take advantage of their gym memberships and get you free trial vouchers.

151 DVD IT

Instead of moping around at home because you haven't got money to pay for a gym, get some friends together and take turns to go to each other's houses and do a fitness DVD. Choose different ones at each house and you'll enjoy the variety of the workout. Arrange with a friend or two to each buy a different DVD and swap around so you don't get bored of doing the same workout.

152 GET LEISURELY

Local leisure centres or university facilities are usually pretty easy on your pocket, and they often have great facilities at a fraction of the price of the gym chains. Check out their memberships too, which can often make them even more economical.

153 MAKE AN INVESTMENT

Before you pay expensive membership fees and tie yourself into a contract with a gym, consider that 20 per cent of those who join gyms in January have stopped going by June and 20 per cent more by December. Before you pay your money, make sure you will have the time and inclination to use the facilities.

154 MAKE IT A NEW YEAR

January is the peak time for joining gyms, so they're all desperately competing for business and offering things such as free digital cameras or MP3 players, no joining fees, two for one memberships or a month free. Take advantage of the fact that they are competing to play them off against one another.

155 JOIN YOUR KIDS

If you have children, don't just watch them play. Join them for a game of tag, play soccer or cycle or walk round the park. Or just put music on at home and dance around the kitchen with them – cheaper than a gym and more fun too.

156 KEEP IT SHORT

The major flaw when joining gyms is the contract length. Sign up and you're often expected to pay for the whole year, even if you stop going. This is much more expensive than it seems, as often you will have to pay a joining fee as well. See if you can have a shorter contract if you're not sure. Often, they are more expensive but you may be able to barter a refund if you then move on to a longer one.

157 GIVE IT UP

Cigarettes, tobacco and cigars are expensive habits as well as unhealthy ones. Giving up will help your finances in the short and long term, as you are far less likely to suffer expensive medical problems later on if you give up now.

158 DRINK LESS

Not only is alcohol in large quantities not good for you, it's highly calorific and expensive too. Make two or three nights a week alcohol free and you'll notice the difference in your health as well as your wallet.

159 GET OUTSIDE

If you want to stay fit but you just can't afford that gym membership anymore, it doesn't mean you have to give up your workouts. Simply invest in a few cheap sets of weights, find some stairs or a hill and do your thing! Or join a local sports club instead, which is cheaper than a gym.

160 BE SENSIBLE

If you may be moving house or undergoing a lifestyle change that may affect your ability to get to the health club or gym, think twice about signing up to a long, non-refundable contract. Simply cutting payments could impact your credit score, so it's important to communicate with them about getting a better deal.

161 MASSAGE YOUR MONEY

If you usually get a massage once a week, cut your bills in half by asking your masseur if they can offer you any home massage tips. Go to the masseur once every two weeks, and during the other week do self-massage and stretching.

162 HAGGLE

Most gyms and health clubs employ a commission-driven sales team to help sign up new members. For you, this is good news because it means they're flexible. Never take the first thing they offer you and always try to get extras, such as a reduction in joining fees or free guest passes (which you could sell to friends).

163 WORK DISCOUNT?

Before you pay out privately for a gym or health club, ask your Human Resources department at work if they have linked deals or discounts. Many medium or larger employers have deals with fitness chains.

164 DON'T WASTE MONEY

Some fitness products aren't worth buying, no matter how low the price. Don't buy herbal supplements or other products that claim to give fitness benefits overnight or promise to melt away pounds without diet and exercise. If it sounds too good to be true, it probably is, so save your money and workout the sensible way.

165 WALK IT OUT

With a little foresight, activities you may take for granted can become part of your exercise routine. Whenever you can, try to walk instead of driving or taking public transport – a 20-minute brisk walk is as good as a workout if you keep the pace up. (Be sure to wear appropriate shoes.)

166 WORK OUT AT HOME

Make the household chores into a workout. Mow the lawn, weed the garden, rake the leaves or shovel the snow. Even indoor activities, such as vacuuming and scrubbing, count as a workout if you increase your heart rate. Put some music on and ramp it up.

167 SET SOME TARGETS

If you were working out in a gym you'd have regular targets to meet, so if you're doing your own fitness schedule at home, don't forget to set goals and deadlines and reward yourself for reaching them just as you would with a trainer. That way, you're less likely to give up.

168 GAME ON

Some of the newer games consoles have games that are designed to get you moving and keep you fit. If a friend or family member already owns a console, why not arrange a loan or swap of the console a few times a week and invest in a fitness game of your own?

169 BOOT CAMP

A fitness boot camp is an outdoor group exercise class that mixes traditional callisthenics and body weight exercises with interval training and strength training. Often, they are much cheaper than other fitness classes and are a great way to keep fit and socialize.

170 SPIN IT OFF

If you can't afford the cost of a gym membership, you probably won't be able to stretch to your own exercise bike either, but there are 'turbo trainer' machines you can buy fairly cheaply that turn your own bike into a home exercise spinner by propping up the back wheel.

171 IMPROVISE

If you'd rather not spend a penny on exercise equipment, use ordinary household items like cans of food or milk or water jugs for weights, tights (panty hose) or stockings for resistance bands and step stools or even planks of wood for step training.

172 PARK FURTHER AWAY

If you travel to work by car, instead of driving right to the door start parking further away so you have to walk. Aim for at least 15 minutes' walking. That way you'll save money on fuel as well as avoiding paying for workouts, because a 30-minute walk a day is great exercise.

173 BUY SECOND-HAND

Some sporting goods stores specialize in used equipment, or you can check out listings for exercise equipment in the local newspaper or charity (thrift) stores. You may also find great deals on used exercise equipment online, just make sure the delivery cost won't put the item out of your budget as they are often very heavy.

174 PUT YOUR FOOT IN IT

Running is a great low-cost workout, but getting the right shoes is imperative if you want to avoid injury. However, the best shoes aren't necessarily the most expensive. Research has shown that mid-price running shoes perform as well as high-cost ones as long as they are fitted correctly, so visit a specialist store for advice.

175 PUMP IT OUT

Instead of spending money joining a gym, invest in some second-hand boxing equipment such as gloves, a punch bag and skipping rope and do your own home workouts a few times a week. Hang the bag in the garage or a bedroom, but if you don't have room then shadow boxing (against the air) is a great workout too.

176 BE WARY OF REPEAT VISITS

Health practitioners such as chiropractors and osteopaths often encourage you to visit them for 'maintenance' sessions every few months. Before you agree, make sure you are certain you really need to see them and it's not just a way of them keeping their money rolling in.

177 SHARE A TRAINER

If you can't afford a personal trainer all to yourself, see if you can find a friend or even a group of friends who will share the cost of a session. This also means you'll have a workout buddy when the trainer isn't there and you'll be spending less money too.

178 BE A GENERALIST

Try to avoid products that focus on one body part, such as the thighs. There's no such thing as 'spot reducing', so for weight loss and general fitness you are better off doing general exercise that doesn't require costly equipment, such as walking, running or cycling.

179 HAVE A BALL

One of the best, and also least expensive, pieces of home exercise equipment is a stability ball. This is an extra-large, inflatable ball that is designed to improve balance and posture while targeting specific muscle groups. You can even use it while you're watching TV.

180 ADD WEIGHT TO YOUR WORKOUT

If you want to add an element of difficulty to your existing workout, without having to exercise for longer, try adding weights, such as an exercise vest or ankle or wrist weights. These can help increase the intensity of your workout without costing you megabucks.

181 TOWEL DOWN

If you do yoga, Pilates or other stretching at home, you don't need to buy expensive equipment. Try using ordinary household equipment instead. For instance, a rolled up towel is just as good as a bolster and a piece of cheap foam or vinyl can be used as a mat.

medical & pharmacy

182 GET WELL AT WORK

Did you know that you may be able to cut health-care premium costs by participating in wellness programmes at your place of work? In countries like the USA almost half of large companies now offer a plan that gives cash rewards or credits towards premiums to employees who meet certain healthy criteria for body mass index, who take steps to lower blood pressure and cholesterol or who work out regularly.

183 FOCUS ON THE WEB

The Internet is a great place to buy prescription glasses, and many sites offer free returns if you don't like your frames. Better still, choose frames you like in a store then find them cheaper online and you could save up to 90 per cent of the cost. You will need to have a prescription from an optician for the lenses.

184 MAKE A SPECIAL TRIP

Comparison shop between supermarkets and pharmacies for essential items like headache tablets and toiletries. Non-grocery items can often be a lot more expensive at supermarkets than at 'dedicated' shops like pharmacies and drugstores. It may be convenient to buy your contact lens solution at the supermarket, but you'll probably get a better price at the pharmacy or optician.

185 ACTIVE SAVVY

Instead of going for big-name drugs and medications, which can be expensive, ask your pharmacist for cheaper alternatives with the same active ingredient and you could make big savings.

186 PREVENT, DON'T CURE

Make a prevention resolution – maintain a healthy body weight, don't smoke, drink sensibly and take regular exercise. This resolution is a good idea if you want to avoid situations in the future that could lead to major health bills.

187 MAX YOUR MEDS

If you know you are going to need your medications for a long time, ask your doctor to prescribe the most medication he/she can. So, for instance, if you have asthma and need ongoing prescriptions for inhalers, ask the doctor to prescribe you three months' instead of one months' worth and save on any pharmacy charges.

188 GET A CERTIFICATE

Many countries run prescription certificates that help you spread the cost of prescription payments over three months or a year. If you use more than 15 prescriptions a month on average, this will probably be a good choice.

189 GO SUPER

The biggest saving is in switching from branded to generic products, regardless of where you shop, but you could gain even more price savings by visiting a discount store or website rather than your usual pharmacy. If you are choosing products from websites, always go for an established brand.

190 DON'T BE DEFENSIVE

If you are in a system where you pay for your own healthcare, like the USA, make sure you avoid what is known as 'defensive medicine'. These are tests and services that you might not actually need, but that are there to cover the doctor's back. Ask lots of questions about why the tests are being done, if they are really necessary, and what your options are.

191 CHECK COSTS

In some countries, including the UK, quite a few people are entitled to free prescription drugs and treatments. Check with the relevant authorities and make sure that you aren't paying if you don't have to.

192 HEALTH ACCOUNT

If you live in a medical fee-paying culture, like the USA, consider getting a health savings account – a savings account that can be used for medical expenses. This type of account has very good tax savings attached, so it's an ideal way to help save for your future medical costs.

193 GET IT O-T-C

Before you pay out for prescription charges, make sure you check to see if you can buy the same medication over the counter for less money. Your pharmacist should be very helpful, so ask them for advice.

184 DRIVE A BARGAIN

In health-care systems or private hospitals, where you have to pay your own costs, both doctors and hospitals will usually negotiate and sometimes adjust their bills based on patient needs, ability to pay cash and other factors. Don't be afraid to ask.

185 DON'T FALL FOR SCAMS

Be careful if you are looking for cheaper medications – most of the 'cheap' options you receive through your e-mail inbox won't be from reputable sources and the drugs they offer are likely to be from the unregulated side of the market, which means they could be dangerous. Don't endanger your life just to help your pocket.

186 REHAB AND RECOVERY

If you're recovering from surgery and facing rehab, following the recovery regimen diligently is a great way to maximize healing and reduce long-term (and possibly costly) effects, as incomplete healing can lead to re-injury or permanent disability. Now is the time to do what your doctors say!

187 GET ORGANIZED

Many people are sloppy about keeping copies of prescriptions, test results, insurance claims and the like. If you have your documents in order it will be easier to win a disagreement with an insurance company, and it can lead to more efficient appointments with your doctor.

188 LOOK AT YOURSELF

Practising self-examination and getting appropriate health screening is a great way to help prevent long and costly medical care as you get older. Work out a schedule for preventive health screening that is appropriate for your age and gender with your health-care provider.

189 DO YOUR HOMEWORK

Know what your medical benefits cover. You need to know what your benefits are before you can use them appropriately, and this includes countries with free healthcare systems. Before you get care, know what you are entitled to and who to approach if you don't feel you're getting it.

200 FIGHT DENIAL

Experts say that 70 per cent of health-insurance claim appeals are successful, particularly in countries like the USA, which has an insurance-based system. If your insurer refuses your claim, don't take it at face value – start an appeal.

201 TRY A SAMPLE

If you are about to start a new drug regime it might be possible to ask your doctor for samples so that you can try the medication free of charge for a few weeks, or even months, to check it works for you before you invest. This will depend on the rules in your health-care system.

202 MEASURE YOUR EYES

If you plan to buy glasses online, remember that you will need to know the distance between your pupils, your 'PD' (Pupillary Distance) so that the lenses are centred in the frame. Websites usually detail methods to find it, but to get the most accurate measurement it's best to ask your optician when you get your eyes tested.

203 TAKE CARE WITH GLASSES

Be careful when ordering glasses online because, depending on which company you choose, you are not necessarily guaranteed a refund or exchange. It's better to pay a bit more and choose an online retailer who offers a refund or exchange.

204 STAY WELL

The simplest way to save money on health care is to stay well. Women who are extremely overweight have annual medical costs that are nearly 70 per cent higher than normal-weight women, so it really does pay to keep yourself in shape.

205 CUT THE PRICE OF VITAMINS

Online websites can offer cut-price deals on vitamins and homeopathic medicines, but look for accredited suppliers or the source brand and always choose branded goods. Some supermarkets may offer discounts online that they wouldn't instore.

206 RENEW WITH CONFIDENCE

When it comes to renewing their health coverage, around 60 per cent of employees just take the company's default plan or check the 'same as last year' box, but that can be a costly mistake. Look at the whole family's finances and see if you can work out a way to make the whole lot cheaper.

dental treatments

207 INSURE YOURSELF

If you aren't having a lot of dental work done, a sensible alternative to buying dental cover is to self-insure. For instance, instead of paying a set amount into a dental insurance plan, stash the money away in a high-interest savings account and use it to pay as you go. And if you don't need it, you can hang on to it and accrue more interest.

208 BRUSH TWICE A DAY

Prevention is better than cure. Spend at least five minutes thoroughly brushing your teeth every night before bed. Brushing properly at night is more important than brushing in the morning, as food stagnates in your mouth overnight producing acid that damages your teeth.

209 SEE A STUDENT

If you are worried about the cost of dental treatment, ask at your local dental school or at your dentists if they run cheaper student programmes, where nearly or newly qualified dentists could treat you (under supervision) at a lower cost. This can often be a good choice for less complicated dental work.

210 DENTAL CLOSURE

If your teeth are prone to cavities and you find your dental bills are really high, why not ask your dentist about some of the new treatments available to help strengthen weak teeth? Dental sealants and fluoride treatments can help in some cases.

211 BE A TOURIST

If you are in need of major private treatment, it's often much cheaper to find a dentist outside your country who'll charge a fraction of the cost. Mexico, Canada and Eastern Europe are popular destinations but this can be a risky option. If something goes wrong, you may have no recourse to remedy the situation. There are many online 'dental tourism' guides but be sure the clinic you choose is properly accredited.

212 CHECK YOUR EMPLOYER

Before you pay out for expensive dental bills or for your own private dental insurance, make sure your employer doesn't offer benefits. Although you will still pay tax on dental plan benefits, it's almost always cheaper than doing it yourself.

213 ROUTINE FLOSSING

Flossing is recommended after brushing as it takes care of the remaining 40 per cent of plaque between your teeth where your brush can't reach. A good dental hygiene routine is the best way to reduce dental costs.

214 DOUBLE-CHECK

The older you are the more expensive your dental cover is likely to be, so if you are older you need to make doubly sure you're getting the best deal you can. Opting for a policy that carries an excess (you may pay for 25 per cent of treatment up to a set limit) is usually cheaper.

215 BE A SAVVY SNACKER

It's not the amount of sugar you eat that could give you expensive teeth problems, it's how often. Eating all of those chocolate treats in one go and rinsing afterwards is actually better than having one every half an hour all day.

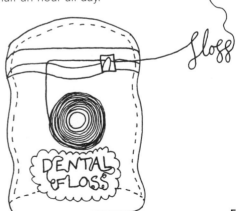

216 KNOW WHAT'S COVERED

Dental plans will mostly pay for general dental treatment, injuries and emergency work, plus they usually cover oral diseases. Cosmetic dentistry, like teeth whitening, porcelain veneers and dental implants, isn't usually covered so remember that.

217 GET COVERED

Many dentists encourage their private patients (especially new patients) to sign up to 'capitation' plans, which spread the cost of your dental care over a year. This can be a great way to make dentistry affordable, especially for large one-off bills. Budget capitation plans are also available, which only cover routine and preventative work.

218 DENTAL DISCLOSURE

Disclosing tablets are coloured pills that dye the plaque left on your teeth after brushing so you can see the spots you're missing. Ask your dentist for some or buy them over the counter and use them every few months to make sure you're not missing danger areas that could cause expensive cavities.

household bills

219 READ THE SMALL PRINT

Whatever energy plan you sign up to, remember the energy company is there to make a profit not to be charitable, so check the small print for exit penalties, capped pricing and other sticking points, like what happens if the price of raw fuel goes down.

220 SEE DOUBLE

Fitting double glazing is a great way to reduce your heating bills because it helps insulate your home. Look for offers from new window stores, especially in the sales. It will probably also get you savings on home insurance.

221 OPEN THE WINDOW

Air-conditioning units are big power drains. Make sure you only turn them on when you need to – try to open doors and windows to get a through-draft instead, and minimize air conditioning to the rooms you really need it in.

222 GET A REBATE

According to a British company that specializes in getting tax refunds, one in three of the UK's 30 million taxpayers may be due a tax rebate. This can equate to money that is yours, but isn't actually in your hands or your bank account. Make sure you seek advice or check with your tax department to see if you could benefit from a tax refund.

223 LEAVE IT ON

It takes a lot of energy to keep switching a boiler (furnace) or air conditioner on or off, so try to set your thermostat to a regular temperature – ideally 18°C (65°F) – and leave it there. Turning it on and off all the time could turn out to be a false economy.

224 GO DIRECT

Simply switching to paying your bills by direct debit instead of cheque or credit card is a great way to save money as most suppliers now charge for non-direct debit payments. It is also a great way to help manage your money if you choose the monthly payment option.

225 CLEAN YOUR OVEN

Cooking in a dirty oven is not only annoying, it's also inefficient. Your oven works best when it's clean, and the best way to keep it clean is to wipe it over regularly from the very first time you use it. If you've inherited a dirty oven, hiring an oven-cleaning company is probably a good investment in terms of energy saving.

226 DRESS WARMLY

Instead of ramping the heating up the moment the temperature drops a few degrees, dress differently at home. Get used to wearing a jumper (sweater) and socks around the house before you start paying out for heating bills.

227 READ YOUR METER

Get to know your electricity meter – for a couple of months, read the meter every week and see if a pattern emerges. Then, try to implement a few energy-saving strategies (like turning lights off when you leave a room) and see how much difference they make. Aim to keep reducing your readings.

228 SEARCH THE NET

There are now specialized companies on the Web who will search through the energy companies for you to help secure the best deal based on your individual circumstances. Visit one for advice and also to check for exclusive online deals. Online deals could save you up to 20 per cent.

229 INSULATE YOUR LOFT

Before the winter, when the heating costs for your home could spiral, make sure you check your loft insulation. Many old houses have little or none, and it could save you as much as a third on your heating bills.

230 DON'T LAG BEHIND

If you have a hot-water tank, letting it stand unlagged (without insulation) is like throwing money into the wind. Combination boilers (furnaces) are usually cheaper, but if you have a water tank make sure you're keeping the heat in with good lagging.

231 TURN IT DOWN

Did you know that turning down your heating thermostat by just one degree could make an 8 per cent difference to your heating bill? Most people really won't notice a one-degree change, so why not try it for a while and see if it saves you money.

232 SWITCH IT OFF

Get into the habit of turning off lights when you leave a room – many of us leave all the lights on in the house even if we're only using one room. If it makes you feel better, use a hall light as a general light so it isn't dark. Never turn on lights unless you really need to.

233 COMPLAIN IN WRITING

If you're making a complaint about something, beware of making a phone call as they are often charged at higher rates and you could spend a long time on the phone. Instead, write or e-mail and ask them to call you to discuss the issue.

234 TOUCH OF THE CLOTH

Instead of spending money on paper table napkins, buy cloth napkins instead. You can wash them with your usual laundry and use them over and over again, which works out far less expensive. They're more stylish too.

235 BOIL WHAT YOU NEED

How many times have you filled the kettle up to the brim before boiling it, rather than just putting in what you need? Heating a kettle full of water uses far more electricity, and what's the point of boiling all that water if you're only going to let most of it go cold anyway?

236 TURN IT OFF EARLY

The heat that food absorbs while it's in the oven keeps it cooking for several minutes after you've taken it. So make the most of this and turn the oven off a few minutes early. It might not sound like much, but two minutes a day over the course of a year could add up to significant electricity or gas savings.

237 SAVE THE PENNIES

Simply switching your energy supplier could save you money, especially if you've never switched before. Compare all the suppliers you can to find the best deal for you and make sure you repeat the process every year to ensure you stay on the cheapest deal.

238 MINIMIZE YOUR TAXES

Local government tax is something we all have to live with, but in some cases people are entitled to lower premiums or even not to pay at all. Check with your local authority about who is exempt or can claim reductions.

239 MONITOR YOUR METER

Keep on top of meter readings to make sure your bills are being calculated correctly and also to note any changes in your usage that might highlight areas for savings.

240 SHUT IT DOWN

When you've finished working for the night, make sure you shut down your computer rather than leaving it on. You're not going to look at it while you sleep, so why waste the money you're paying to keep it on?

241 BUNDLE YOUR SERVICES

A great way to save money on your energy bills is to get all your energy from the same supplier. So find one that will supply both your gas and electricity and hunt around for the best deal they can do for you.

242 SEAL YOUR FRIDGE

Refrigerators and freezers use a lot of power and they can quickly become inefficient. Check your seals with a piece of paper – if the paper falls out when the door is shut, your seals need replacing.

water rates & charges

243 USE LESS WATER

There are some simple ways to reduce your water bill (and it's better for the environment as well). A bath uses 80 litres (21 gallons) of water while a shower uses just 30 litres (8 gallons); brushing your teeth with the tap running uses 10 litres (2½ gallons), which is more than the 9 litres (2¼ gallons) used when you flush the toilet.

244 A BIG BUTT

Gardening is a big water user, taking up a staggering 450 litres (119¼ gallons) in just one hour. Save water in the garden by collecting rainwater in a water butt so you don't have to use your hose. Give plants a summer soaking once or twice a week rather than watering daily.

245 DO A BEDROOM COUNT

As a general rule, if you have more bedrooms than people in your home you could probably save by going on to a water meter. If you request a water meter, most suppliers will install it at no cost and you will be charged for your exact usage. Most water companies also offer the right to switch back to an unmeasured charge within the first 12 months.

246 FIT A DEVICE

To help save water in your home, fit a save and flush device to your toilet, which can reduce the amount of water you use flushing your toilet by half. So, if you flush ten times a day, that's 45 litres (12 gallons) of water saved.

247 FILL IT UP

Make sure you only use the washing machine, dishwasher and tumble dryer when they are full. This makes them much more efficient and will lower your bills.

248 SHOWER OFF

Try to take showers instead of baths, as you're likely to use less than half the water of a bath, especially if you have a big tub and like to have it full. Save baths for a once-a-week wind down and shower at other times.

driving

249 DON'T BE A NEWBIE

New cars depreciate fastest in their earliest years and the minute a new car is driven off the forecourt it is estimated to lose 25 per cent of its value. If you are looking to buy a car, opt for one that is 18 months to two years old for the best value.

250 GET IN LINE

Get your wheel alignment checked regularly. If the wheels are out of line it can make tyres wear unevenly and need replacing sooner.

251 GET TWO-WHEEL DRIVE

Four-wheel drive cars are expensive to buy and expensive to run, so if you don't really need one investing in a two-wheel drive instead will save you money. If you really must buy one, try to opt for a model with optional four-wheel drive so you can save running costs where possible.

252 GO CLASSIC

In many countries (like the UK), there are tax breaks on classic cars over a certain age, and they are good investment vehicles because they keep their value. They can be expensive to run, however, so are better suited to being a second car rather than for everyday use.

253 FIND A MECHANIC

Unless your car is still under warranty (and some people get around this by changing their car every few years so it always is) it's essential you have a good mechanic who you can trust not to overcharge you for work. Shop around to find one and ask friends for recommendations.

254 WASH IT YOURSELF

Don't go to the car wash – washing your car yourself is good exercise and it will make you feel great to have saved all that money too. If you have kids, get them involved for a fun family afternoon.

255 GO SPARE

Before you invest in a car that seems cheap at face value, investigate repair and maintenance costs. Some foreign import cars can have very expensive parts, so it could be less efficient in the long run.

256 CHECK TYRE PRESSURES

Tyres are expensive. Keeping them at the right pressure not only makes driving safer, it also extends their life and saves you money. Remember your vehicle manufacturer is likely to recommend different pressures for loaded and unloaded journeys, so check the handbook.

257 LOSE YOUR ROOF BARS

Did you know that driving with roof bars on when you're not using them uses for more fuel because it makes your car less aerodynamic. Make a point of taking roof bars off your car when they are not in use.

258 DON'T PAY FOR EXTRAS

If you want to buy a new car, consider a demonstration model – they cost less than new cars, but have done few miles and are often loaded with the kind of extras you'd normally have to pay for, such as satnav and tinted windows.

259 GO SLOW

Instead of ramping up your speed, bear in mind that driving with low revs and at an even pace is the most effective way to use fuel. Leave lots of room between you and other cars to prevent having to brake and then accelerate fast.

260 PREPARE FOR THE COLD

Buy antifreeze in the summer when it's cheaper. Winterize your car before the cold weather hits – hunt around for snow tyres in advance, get your car serviced and make sure your four-wheel-drive system is working correctly, if you have one (many drivers don't use it at other times of the year).

261 GRAB A BARGAIN

Make sure you don't pay the asking price for a car if you buy it from a garage or dealership. Go with a friend if you feel you might cave in, and always try to get as many added extras as you can. Even asking for a full tank of fuel could save you money.

262 JUMP AHEAD

If your car is more than a few years old, there's always the chance that one day it won't start. It's a good investment to keep a pair of inexpensive jump leads in the boot (trunk) so you can restart it yourself rather than paying for an expensive towing service.

263 KEEP IT LIGHT

It's tempting to let the junk accumulate in the back of your car or use it for storage, but bear in mind that the heavier load you drive around, the less efficient your car is on fuel costs. Keep it as light as possible.

264 BUY LIGHTWEIGHT

Buying a lightweight car means you can lower your running costs. Not only does it use less fuel but it's also cheaper on oil, because you don't have to buy the expensive 'engine cleaning' variety like you do with more expensive cars.

265 CHECK YOUR OIL AND WATER

Don't be tempted to leave off servicing your car until it needs repair – maintenance is always the most cost-effective option. Oil and water are essential for your car's engine so make sure you top them up regularly.

266 CLEAN UP

Instead of buying expensive car shampoos and chrome cleaners, use normal washing-up (dishwashing) liquid to clean bodywork and clean chrome with vinegar then soap, rinse well and polish with newspaper for a cheap, professional shine.

267 BUY ON PRICE

There's no real evidence that any type of petrol (gasoline) is better than any other, so buy on price. Supermarkets often have really good prices on fuel and you can fill up while you are doing your weekly shop, meaning one less journey.

car insurance

268 DRIVE ALONE

As a general rule, the more named drivers you have on your car insurance (particularly if they are young), the more you will pay. Stick to just you (and a partner, if necessary) to keep insurance premiums down.

269 KEEP COSTS LOW

There are loads of tricks to help keep your car insurance low. Upping the amount you pay in excess, not making a claim for minor things like scratches to the paintwork, parking off the road, and avoiding picking up driving violations will all help to lower your quote.

270 BE ACCURATE

Be as accurate as you can about your mileage – giving your car insurer a mileage that is higher than you actually do could increase your premium for no reason. If you are a low-mileage user, limiting your mileage is another way to bring down costs but you must be sure you can stay within the limit.

271 SWAP INSURERS

If you have a car, insurance is a necessary expense. However, don't just stay with your provider because it's the easy option. Shopping around could save you a significant amount and it's definitely better to pay for it all in one lump sum than to go for a monthly deal. Car insurers can charge as much as 23 per cent APR.

272 VOLUNTEER

Contact your car insurer and offer a voluntary excess, which is the amount you will have to pay towards each claim before the insurers pay out. Work out what you could afford if you had to make a claim and volunteer that to lower your premiums.

273 PROTECT YOURSELF

If you have built up a long history of not claiming on your insurance policy your insurance company should give you a bonus. But make sure they also offer no claims protection, which is a small premium you pay to ensure you keep your no claims bonus even if you have to make a claim.

274 CHOOSE SAFETY FIRST

The more secure your car is, the lower your car insurance premium will be. Keeping it in a garage is best, then off-street parking, but if your car is parked on a busy street your premium will be higher. Certain postcodes (zipcodes) are more expensive too, so check out your options first.

275 SHOP AROUND

If you're buying a new car, it's tempting to take the quick and easy option and opt for the insurance offered to you on the forecourt. Don't be fooled by the salesperson, however, as these deals are rarely as good as you can get if you shop around, you are likely to be paying around 30 per cent more.

276 LEAVE IT PLAIN

If you want to save money on your car insurance, steer clear of modifications to your car that might boost your premium. Supercharging the engine and even adding customized paintwork to the outside could mean you pay more.

shopping savings

277 GO IT ALONE

The best way to save money on groceries is to go shopping once a week without your children so you can really concentrate on getting things right. There's nothing more likely to make you grab items you don't need and rush out of the store than a child who's misbehaving.

278 THINK LOCAL

It's a myth that supermarkets are cheaper for everything. For bulk goods, yes, but it's worth checking your local fruit and vegetable store and butcher, as often their prices for fresh produce are cheaper.

279 BUY JIT

Because food is perishable, it's worth borrowing a principle from big businesses – buy things just in time (JIT). So, apart from a few staples, make sure your don't have food sitting around that will go off before you can use it.

280 REACH FOR IT

Supermarkets usually put the premium brands between knee and shoulder height, with the highest markup items positioned at chest level, so you instinctively and easily grab the higher-priced items. Take a look at the shelves in your supermarket and reach to get the cheaper products.

281 BUY IN BULK

The more of something you buy in one go, the cheaper it will be per unit. Buying in bulk (as long as you know you will use the food and not waste it) is a great way to save money on your shopping, and it saves on packaging too that means it's a greener way to shop. Look for things like baby wipes, fruit juice, toilet paper and bottled water.

282 BE CANNY

Keep track of the convenience foods you regularly rely on (like pasta sauces, canned tomatoes, baby foods and so on) and see if you can come up with a lower-cost alternative. Supermarket own-brands can be a real money saver, but can be hit or miss on the taste scale. You'll have to experiment to find the ones you like.

283 SHARE IT

A great way to save money on buying in bulk is to share the costs with a friend, neighbour or family member. Make a list of the things you would all benefit from buying in bulk and see if you can buy it together to make savings.

284 GET A MAP

Next time you are in your local supermarket, get a store map (or draw one if they don't have them). Then, when you make your next shopping list, do it in order according to the map. Not only will it make your shopping trip quicker, you'll be less likely to buy extras.

285 EAT UP

Never go grocery shopping when you're tired or hungry, because you'll be more likely to buy things you don't need and that aren't on your list, or to buy too much of something. Have a snack before you go and try to shop mid-morning when you're less likely to be hungry.

286 BE A POTATO HEAD

Potatoes are a great, cheap, staple food, and they're particularly economical if you buy a big bag. Even if you end up not being able to use the last few before they go bad, you'll still have made huge savings. Check out your local farm store as they are often cheaper for large bags than supermarkets.

287 WRITE A STAPLE LIST

Keep a list of household storecupboard staples – such as spices, canned tuna and beans, flour, sugar, soy sauce, mayonnaise and mustard – next to your shopping list. Then, even if you haven't got them on your list that week you can take advantage if you see them on special offer.

288 BET ON A BUTCHER

If you want to eat good meat at a fraction of the supermarket cost, your local butcher could be your new best friend. Offering cheaper cuts of meat than supermarkets, and with the knowledge to give you advice on how to make the most of your meat, getting to know your butcher is a great way to save.

289 TAKE A CALCULATOR

If your mobile (cell) phone hasn't got a calculator and your mental arithmetic just isn't up to working out those sale savings, take a calculator with you to the store. For instance, it's usually cheaper to buy bigger cans, but if smaller cans are in the bargain bin it may be cheaper to buy these instead.

290 SHOP ONCE A WEEK

Fewer trips to the store mean fewer chances to load up on things you don't need. Go just once a week and you'll have time to comparison-shop for the best prices (look at the unit prices listed on the shelf for the most accurate comparisons) and to scan the aisles for those bargain offers that are too good to miss.

291 ORDER ONLINE

Shopping online for your groceries is a great way to save money, as you're less likely to yield to the sort of tempting offers supermarkets are so good at dangling in front of you. Plus it's only a short walk to the kitchen to see if you really need that extra item.

292 CHOOSE THE END OF DAY

The last hour before the store closes is one of the best times to shop. Check out the end-of-day chill cabinet for sale-price items. You can get significant markdowns on meat if you buy things that are about to expire – either cook them that evening or freeze them.

293 FIND SOME BALANCE

Saving money on your grocery shopping is about making changes you will hardly notice, not those that will make you miserable. Don't expect to make all your changes overnight – be prepared to experiment for a few months to find your balance.

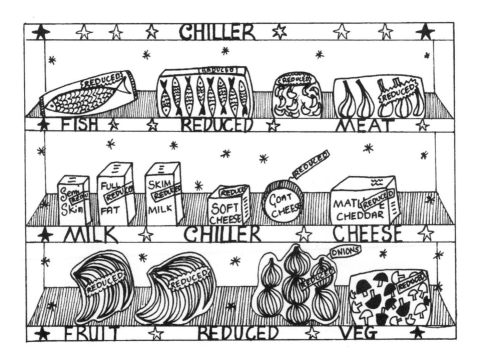

294 ALTERNATE STORES

It's tempting to go to the same store every time because it's usually quicker and easier, but don't be afraid to shop around. You will probably find that certain goods are cheaper in some stores, so try to alternate your shopping trips and shop around to take this into account.

295 REWARD YOUR LIST

If you've just started shopping from a list, it can feel a bit limiting, and perhaps even boring. Until you get used to sticking to a list it's worth reminding yourself why you're doing it. When you get back from your shopping trip, write down all the things that you might have bought if you hadn't taken a list along and work out how much money you've saved!

296 SHOP ON A MONDAY

Mondays are a good choice for budget shoppers as supermarkets often have more items on special offer that day. Get to know when your favourite stores discount so that you can take advantage of it.

cook up a storm

297 DOWNSHIFT

A great way to save money is to start experimenting with different levels of your most used foods. For example, if you usually buy the most expensive bread (organic, hand baked, etc.), try moving down a level to mass produced versions. Or if you usually buy a cheap brand, try moving down to own-brand goods and see if you can tell the difference. Experiment to see which areas you can comfortably downshift in – you might be willing to use cheaper toilet paper, for instance, but not fruit juice or breakfast cereal.

298 MAKE MEAT COUNT

When you eat meat, choose recipes that spread the wealth. Pasta and rice meat dishes are filling, and you can often get away with using small portions of meat without sacrificing flavour. Asian food, such as stir-fries, are also a healthy and inexpensive way to make meat count.

299 COOK FOOD FROM SCRATCH

Pre-prepared foods are more expensive than cooking food from scratch. If you've got a prepared food habit, try to limit yourself to one or two nights a week and cook fresh food the rest of the time.

300 FREEZE UP

If you're not sure you'll use your leftovers within a few days, because you've got other food you have to use up, put them in the freezer instead of the fridge and they'll last months rather than days. If you eat a lot of toast, keep sliced bread in the freezer (thick sliced is better), this way you'll never waste bread and it can be toasted in minutes straight from the freezer.

301 COOK AND KEEP

Make it a rule to try and cook once to eat twice and make everything you cook enough for two meals or more. This means cooking double quantities of things like pasta sauces, then all you have to do is prepare some pasta or vegetables to have with it the following night.

302 RESCUE YOUR BREAD

If your loaf of bread has dried out, dip it in cold water and then put it in a warm oven for a few minutes, or until the outside is crisp and the inside soft. Don't turn the oven on just to do this though, do it when you've got something else cooking otherwise you won't be saving!

303 HAVE A USE-UP MONTH

Every now and again – probably twice a year is best – have a 'use-up' month where you try to buy the minimum you need and aim to use up all the food in your fridge and cupboards. Plan ahead to do this at a time when you haven't got a lot of other pressures, because you might need to be more creative.

304 UPSIDE DOWN IT

When your sauce and condiment bottles are close to being empty, stand them upside down overnight so that all the dregs settle at the lid end – this way it's easier to scrape out everything that's left. For the last little bits, use a drop of vinegar to wash it out.

305 CALCULATE YOUR SAVINGS

Don't underestimate the amount of money that making small weekly savings can add up to. Think about it in relation to one item, say a bag of pasta, and see how much you save by switching to a different brand. Think of how this adds up over a whole year. If you can make similar savings on many of your staple items, that's a whole load of savings.

306 BLEND A PÂTÉ

If you have leftover meat or fish, blitz it in the food processor and turn it into a pâté. You can add some butter and a little cream, sprinkle in some herbs and have it on toast for lunch.

307 BIG-BATCH COOKING

Choose easy recipes that you can make in big batches and freeze for later. Soups are convenient, low-cost and versatile and make nourishing time-saving meals. Freeze a basic broth to which you can add different ingredients as you like.

308 BE A SMOOTHIE

Instead of using fresh fruit in your smoothies, why not use frozen – raspberries and blueberries are much less expensive if you buy them frozen and they won't spoil. Also, take advantage of seasonal low prices by freezing your own fresh fruit – arrange it on a tray to freeze, then bag it up when frozen to avoid 'clumping'.

308 CLEAR OUT THE FRIDGE

If you find yourself throwing a lot of food away, aim to have a weekly (or monthly) 'clear out the fridge' night, where you use everything you would otherwise have to throw away. Not only will you save money on food wastage, it will also help you to get creative in the kitchen!

310 USE IT STALE

Don't throw away stale bread – it's great for making breadcrumbs to use in meatballs, burgers and meatloaf, as well as herb crusts and vegetarian recipes. If you don't want to use them immediately, just freeze them in airtight bags.

311 HOMEMADE ICES

Instead of throwing away the remnants of soft drinks from cans and bottles, pour them into freezer containers and turn them into homemade ice lollies (ice pops). It doesn't matter if you haven't got enough to fill a whole mould, just top it up when you have some spare soft drinks available for a layered effect.

312 PICK A PICKLE

Jars of pickles and chutneys in the supermarket can be expensive, but they're easy to make at home. Choose fruit and vegetables when they're in season (that is, after all, the way pickling started). Make as much pickle as you can in one go to make it more cost efficient. This way you'll have them throughout the year and may even have enough to give as gifts.

313 GET LOOSE

Loose tea is cheaper than tea bags, so why not try to use loose tea whenever you can? You can even buy an inexpensive insert for your teapot to filter out the leaves, which makes it almost as convenient as bags.

314 SAVE YOUR CHOCOLATE

When you heat chocolate for cooking, don't wash the bowl immediately you've poured it out. Let the chocolate cool and reset, then scrape it out. Use these scrapings to decorate cakes and other desserts, then you won't have to buy expensive toppings.

315 MAKE YOUR OWN MUESLI

Instead of buying 'luxury' muesli from the supermarket, why not buy the separate constituents yourself and mix your own in a large container? Buying in bulk is cheaper and you can make it exactly how you like it.

316 SCENT YOUR SUGAR

If you do a lot of baking, buying a real vanilla pod (bean) might be a good investment. Bury it in a jar of sugar and the delicious vanilla scent will permeate the sugar. You can keep refilling the jar with sugar to make further batches.

317 SNEAK IN SOME CARROT

When making anything with minced (ground) meat add a grated carrot or two to it bulk out. This makes the meal more cost-effective and is a really good way of sneaking in some extra vegetables. If you add the carrots as you put in the meat they take on the meaty flavour, so you are unlikely to be able to taste them – it's a great money-saving option.

318 SAVE THE FAT

When you roast chicken or beef, save the fat. Pour it into a small container and cover, then store it in the fridge. It lasts for weeks and is delicious used in cooking instead of oils or butter.

319 BUY A BREADMAKER

If your family eats a lot of bread, investing in a breadmaker could be a great way of decreasing your food costs, while at the same time increasing the quality of your diet. Buying separate ingredients, such as flour, oil and yeast, is usually cheaper and always better than the manufactured alternative.

320 PASS THE PASTA

If you're cooking on a budget, especially for a family, think pasta. It's a very filling, high-energy food and is incredibly versatile.

321 POWDER YOUR BAKING

You don't need to use fresh milk for cooking sauces and other baking – use cheaper dried milk or long-life milk instead and you'll be unlikely to taste the difference.

322 REACH FOR THE RICE

Rice is one of the most versatile foods. You can eat it as a main dish, side dish or even dessert. Never make the smallest amount of rice listed on the package – go up a level and have rice pudding for dessert the next day, sauté rice with leftover vegetables or use up stock (broth) for a risotto. Rice can be stored for 1–2 days in a refrigerator, but shouldn't be reheated more than once.

323 USE BEANS

Beans are a great food if you're on a budget – they're full of protein and goodness and are amazingly versatile. Use them to bulk out sauces and casseroles, as a side dish with main meals and even on their own as a summer salad with a tasty dressing.

324 STOCK UP

If you've got a taste for ready-meals (or you like to take them to work to have for lunch) don't buy them each week. Wait until they're on special offer, then stock up and keep them in the freezer.

325 NOODLE KNOW-HOW

Noodles are a cheap and easy way to pad out meals – use them to turn soup into a meal or to add bulk to salads and stir-fries. They are filling, nutritious and take little cooking, which makes them a great budget-lover's choice.

326 SCRAP THE SOUP

Once every few weeks make a soup out of all the odds and ends in your fridge or freezer. Fry a small onion to start with, throw in the odds and ends, add some stock (broth) (preferably homemade) and let it cook for a while – then blitz and eat or store.

lovely leftovers

327 BAN BANANA WASTE

Don't throw away overripe bananas – they are great for making banana bread. If you haven't got time for baking, use them in fruit smoothies or mash them up and freeze into a healthy banana 'ice cream'.

328 TAKE THEM HOME

If you have lunch meetings at work and there are sandwiches, fruit or cookies left over, wrap them up and take them home or leave them in the fridge at work for lunch the next day.

329 MAKE ROAST PATTIES

If you've got leftovers from an oven or pot roast, simply put everything in a food processor, add some breadcrumbs and stock (broth) and make patties. Fry the patties in a little butter or olive oil, melt some cheese on top and serve with salad for a great light lunch.

330 FREEZE YOUR MASH

Freeze leftover mashed potatoes in small amounts in freezer bags, then use them in recipes as a thickening agent in place of flour. You can use one part mashed potatoes to two parts flour in virtually any recipe, from soups and casseroles to homemade bread.

331 CHILL CHILLI

If you've got leftover steak or roast beef, you can make a great quick chilli: chop the meat into small pieces, add some canned kidney beans, chilli powder, chopped tomatoes and passata, bring to the boil and then simmer for an hour or so. Serve with rice or baked potatoes.

332 HAND OUT THE HAM

Ham is a great choice for making leftover meals, because it's got such a distinctive flavour. Ham pie is delicious (especially if you've got chicken too) and ham soup is a good winter choice. You can make ham hash or patties by whizzing it in a food processor or simply slice it and serve with poached eggs for a hearty breakfast.

333 BUY A BLENDER

One of the most important pieces of equipment for budgeting chefs is a blender – great for mixing anything from smoothies, soups and baking dough to chopping vegetables and grinding spices. It is also invaluable for turning all those leftovers into gourmet feasts.

334 PLAN YOUR USE

Get used to using leftovers instead of throwing them away. In fact, stop calling them leftovers and start calling them your next meal! Have a list on the front of the fridge that details what's inside, and every time you put something in add it to the list.

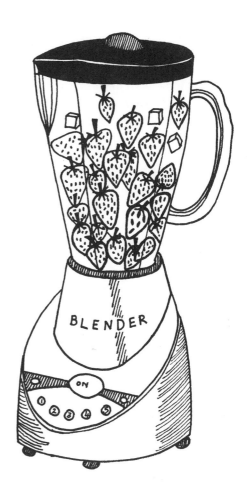

335 MAKE MORE

When you're cooking your evening meal, make an extra portion and pack it up so you can eat it for lunch the next day. This is much cheaper than buying lunch out or making something from scratch, and needs no extra effort.

336 CREATE A STASH CUPBOARD

Keep a cupboard or drawer in your kitchen for freebies: milk and cream pots from coffee bars; salt, pepper and sauce sachets from diners and restaurants; tea, coffee and hot chocolate from hotels; and individual jams and honey, sachets of sugar and straws and napkins. These are great for picnics, lunchboxes and supplementing your own supplies.

337 MAKE BOOZY CUBES

Don't throw away leftover wine – freeze it in ice-cube trays and store in a freezer bag when they are frozen. You can use them when you are cooking – pop a few wine cubes into a sauce for an instant restaurant-style flavour.

338 WRITE THE DATE

Make sure you write the date on your foods when you put your leftovers in the fridge or freezer. Then you can be sure you use them within the right timescale to prevent them going bad or losing their taste.

339 SPICE IT UP

The best way to use leftovers is not to think about just reheating them, but to use them as an ingredient for a whole new recipe. The addition of herbs and spices is a great way to do this – make a great pasta sauce with leftover meat or fish, tomatoes and a sprinkling of basil and oregano.

340 DON'T CHUCK CHICKEN

Chicken is one of the most versatile meats. You start with a roast chicken, and then you can make chicken salad, chicken noodles, pies or pasta sauces. Finally, use the carcass to make a great stock (broth) (add carrot, celery, onion, bay leaves and a bouquet garni, cover with water and simmer for a few hours). You can use it for soup, casseroles or risottos.

341 BAKE SPAGHETTI

For a quick and easy pasta bake, take your leftover pasta and sauce, chop it up, put it in an ovenproof dish with layers of courgettes (zucchini) and aubergines (eggplants), grate some cheese on top and you've got an instant pasta bake for tomorrow's meal.

342 GRIND YOUR MEAT

The most cost-effective way to use minced (ground) meat is to buy as much as you can and use it for a variety of different meals – meat loaves, pasta sauces, pies, chilies, burgers and meatballs – to name just a few.

343 VEG IT UP

Leftover vegetables are great for a midweek brunch. Simply add them to an omelette along with some grated cheese and you've a quick, cheap and easy meal in minutes. Or make some pastry (or use ready-rolled pastry that you've bought on special offer and kept in the freezer) and make a vegetable quiche.

344 SOMETHING SWEET

Don't think you can only use leftovers for main meals, you can make tasty desserts too. Use sweet sauces, such as cranberry sauce, or leftover fruit for cakes and muffins, stale bread for bread and butter pudding, and potato for sweet potato cakes or dumplings.

345 KEEP THE BASICS

The holy trinity of leftover cooking is carrots, celery and onions. Using these three items you can make a casserole out of almost anything. Adding freshly sautéed vegetables freshens and moistens leftover meat so it doesn't feel dry and tough.

346 MAKE USE OF EGGS

Eggs are very versatile and can help you make the most of your leftovers. They are a main ingredient in omelettes and quiches and can be used to bind ingredients together when making burgers and patties. They are also a good source of protein.

347 KEEP SPUD PEELINGS

When you peel potatoes don't throw the peelings away. Put them in a single layer on an oven tray, sprinkle with a little oil, salt, pepper and chilli powder (or whatever seasoning you like) and bake them in the oven at about 200°C (375°F) until they go crispy. Crisps (potato chips) on a budget!

storage secrets

348 KEEP BREAD FRESH

Bread bins (boxes) help keep bread (and other foods, such as cookies and cakes) fresher for longer. They also stop crumbs getting all over the kitchen.

349 STORE WELL

If you grow your own fruit, like apples and pears, you can store them for many months as long as you do it right. If you wrap them in tissue or newspaper and store them in a cool, dark and well-ventilated place they will last for a long time. Don't try to store damaged or bruised fruit as it will go bad and make affect other produce. Check the stored fruit regularly and remove any fruit that is not keeping well.

350 BOWL IT OVER

The best way to keep fruit so it lasts for the longest possible time is to put it in a bowl away from the oven, heat and sunlight. If possible, store bananas in a different bowl as they can cause other fruit to overripen.

351 BAG A SANDWICH

When you buy your fresh fruit and vegetables at the supermarket, save the small bags that you put them in and use them again for your sandwiches. This will stop you having to spend money on sandwich bags and is an environmentally sound way to reuse plastic.

352 BUY ONIONS CHOPPED

If you don't have time to cook things from fresh, make life easier by buying your onions frozen and already chopped. They can be cooked straight from frozen and even though they are more expensive than raw onions, none will go to waste and they are certainly far cheaper than buying ready-made, convenience meals.

353 EVERYTHING IN ITS PLACE

Try to keep separate cupboards or areas for different types of food – one for cereals, one for cans, one for oils, condiments and sauces, one for rice and pasta, and so on. If you do this it will be easier to find everything and you're less likely to forget foods and waste them.

354 FREEZE YOUR MILK

If you find you have too much milk in your fridge (when you're going away on a trip, for example), you can freeze it in unopened plastic cartons to stop it going to waste. Then simply defrost it in the fridge when you want to use it.

355 WATER IT DOWN

When you buy a lettuce, don't just throw it in the fridge. Break it up with your hands and place it in a bowl of cold water; alternatively wash it in icy water and wrap it in a clean, wet tea towel. Stored in either of these ways in the fridge it will stay fresh and crispy for far longer.

356 REPACKAGE IT

Don't forget that buying in bulk is a great way to stock your freezer. For instance, if you have bought a chicken on special offer, repackage it when you get home into cookable portions and freeze until you're ready to use them.

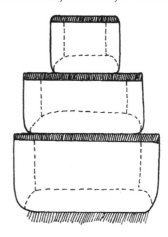

357 JAR IT

It's a good idea to keep rice and pasta in big, clear storage jars – it's easy to see what you have and it keeps it super-fresh for longer. This is especially important if you're buying lots in bulk.

358 FOIL YOUR CHEESE

Cheese will keep better in the fridge if you wrap it in aluminium foil rather than keep it in plastic bags or containers because it stops it sweating and keeps it airtight. Wrap your cheese in foil as soon as you get it home from the store, and reuse the foil as much as you can.

359 BAG YOUR FLOUR

When you first buy flour, you can do a neat storage-lengthening trick. Enclose the bag of flour in an airtight plastic bag and freeze for 24 hours. Remove from the freezer, but leave the plastic bag in place (it has to be airtight for this to work). The cold kills flour mites and bugs and the plastic bag keeps it dry.

360 KEEP THE STEM

If you are only using part of a (bell) pepper, leave the stem, seeds and membrane intact and put it back into the fridge. The pepper will keep for much longer than if you remove them.

361 KEEP COOL

Keep the fridge at a cool 1°–5°C (about 34°–41°F) and your chilled food will stay fresh for longer. The most perishable (and often the most expensive) food is kept in the fridge, so keep an eye on use-by dates. Your freezer and fridge should work hand in hand to help you store food for longer.

362 USE A FREEZER

One of the best investments you can make if you want to save money on food is a freezer. It gives you the space to store food when you buy it on special offer, to keep extra portions of meals you make yourself, and even store 'expensive' foods when you can buy them on offer.

363 VERY SAUCY

Pesto sauce for pasta is a staple choice for fridge and cupboards, but it only lasts a few weeks once it's opened so half a jar often gets thrown away. Instead of wasting it, divide it into teaspoon-sized portions, freeze them individually, and then put them in a freezer container. Keep them frozen and use as and when you want.

364 WRAP UP VEGGIES

To keep them fresher for longer, wrap lettuce, carrots, courgettes (zucchini) and other vegetables in kitchen paper towels, then put them in plastic bags in the salad compartment of the fridge. The paper stops condensation softening the vegetables and prevents mould growth.

menu planning

365 GO SLOW

A slow cooker (stockpot) is a great investment because, as it transmits heat through the food slowly, you can use cheaper cuts of meat and they will still be tender at the end of the cooking process. This method of cooking is great for busy mums or those who work long hours as you can prepare the meal in the morning and come back at night to a perfectly cooked meal.

366 HAVE A MEAL ROUTINE

Most families and households will find that they fall into some sort of routine for their weekly eating. It might run something like: Sunday – roast; Monday – fish; Tuesday – leftovers from roast; Wednesday – pasta; Thursday – casserole; Friday – anything goes (homemade pizzas, going out or fast food etc.); Saturday – stir-fry or noodles. Get into your habit as it will help you to budget and save money.

367 SIMPLE BALANCING ACT

Don't expect to be able to plan a menu from nothing straightaway – when it comes to learning to balance your kitchen books, slow and steady wins the race. Start by simply creating a menu for the week that balances foodstuffs. You'll be amazed at the savings from not buying too much food.

368 ANYTHING GOES

Build flexibility into your menu plan and stick to your thrifty ways by adding an 'anything goes night' to your menu plan. It's a good idea to do this the night before you are due to do your shopping or have it delivered. Basically, it's where you use up all your leftovers and get creative with your cooking.

369 SPECIAL-OFFER CHEF

For a week, scan the food ads and notices for special offers and sales and draft out a week-long menu plan using these items. It might not be something you can do long term, but it's a great way of practising your menu-planning skills.

370 READ YOUR DIARY

When you're planning your menu, you need to take into account your family's schedule. For instance, if someone is home alone one night, they could have leftover omelette or salad, some nights there might be guests for dinner and there's no point buying bread for packed lunches if the children are off school or you're away on business.

371 PLAN YOUR MEALS

Menu planning is the first thing you should do if you want to save money on food bills. Make yourself a promise not to visit the supermarket or food store again until you've made a menu plan, and stick to it!

372 MAKE A LIST

In order to ensure that you only buy food when you need it, laminate a family shopping list that details all of the regular items that you buy. Leave a space underneath for notes for extra items. Using a wipeable marker pen, make it everyone's responsibility to mark what they want/need.

373 KEEP TO THE TRIED AND TESTED

If you love cooking it's fun to experiment with new dishes, but be careful of doing this too often as it can play havoc with budgeting. Stick mainly to dishes that you know how to cook, and only try new dishes once every few weeks or one special night a week. Try rotating your menu every two weeks, so you have 14 different dishes, and that way the family won't get bored.

374 VERSATILITY IS KEY

Great menu planning is all about being versatile. For example, if you've planned a pork or beef roast, but your butcher or supermarket has chickens on special offer, simply change the meat over and stick to the rest of the plan.

375 STOCK UP ON SNACKS

If you have children, particularly if they do sports, it's worth building some hefty snacks into your weekly menu so they don't end up raiding the fridge and ruining your planning. Cheap snacks are potato-, pasta-, bread- or egg-based.

376 RECYCLE THE PLAN

After you've made menu plans for a few weeks, you'll find you can recycle them! Your family won't mind, and you'll save even more time and energy. Plus, as you get to know your plan better, you'll know which quantities to buy in order to save waste.

377 TAKE ADVANTAGE

Once you have all your menu plans, keep them together in one place and then you can use them again. For instance, if you made a menu plan when beef was on special offer a few weeks ago and it comes up on special again, simply reuse the menu plan.

easy savings

378 BUY METAL

When it comes to kitchen pans, buying metal is a great idea even if it costs a little more. Nonstick pans can give short-term savings, but they don't last as long.

379 HAVE A GRATE SANDWICH

To reduce the amount of cheese you use in sandwiches and salads, grate the cheese instead of using slices or chunks. As well as saving you money, it's healthier too.

380 OILY FISH IS A NO-BRAINER

Oily fish are an essential part of a healthy diet, and the best thing it they're not necessarily expensive. Mackerel and sardines are among the cheapest fish you can buy and they're among the best for you too, so it's a no-brainer!

381 SELECT STRONG CHEESE

Cheese can be expensive, so wherever possible use smaller amounts of it. For example, when you are making sauces you can cut the amount of cheese that you use in half by using a strong-tasting, mature cheese, such as Cheddar or Parmesan. Using less cheese will mean that your meals are also lower in fat.

382 GET A THICK BOTTOM

One of the best investments you can make for your kitchen is a good, thick-bottomed saucepan. Not only will it last for many years, saving you the expense of buy replacements, it will cook your food thoroughly and stop it sticking to the bottom, which saves the food from burning and being wasted.

383 PICK A PULSE

Bulk out your meat stews, casseroles or sauces with vegetables and/or pulses, which are cheaper. Lentils and chickpeas are a great choice as they're cheap and contain protein, which boosts the goodness of the meal.

384 BUY SEMI-SKIMMED

Semi-skimmed milk is cheaper than whole milk and is healthier too. Not only is it lower in fat, but because of the fat to water ratio your body actually absorbs the calcium better. However, don't give semi-skimmed milk to children under the age of two, as they need the extra calories.

385 USE LESS FAT

Fats and oils can be expensive so use them sparingly. Try using half your usual amount and only add more if you really need to. You'll soon find you're buying far less oils and fats than you were before.

386 GO VEGGIE

When it comes to oils and fats for cooking, don't use the expensive ones like olive oil or butter. Save these for flavouring and cook with cheaper oils, such as vegetable, rapeseed or canola oils instead. Wherever you can, use nonstick frying pans so you won't need to use as much fat. A good pan is worth the investment, as it will last for many years.

387 GO SEASONAL

Seasonal fruits and vegetables are always cheaper than imported varieties, so try to plan your meals around seasonal produce if you want to get more for your money. Food eaten in season is healthier too, because it will be packed with vitamins and minerals.

388 MAKE THE CUT

You don't need more than two knives in your kitchen (one big, one small), as long as they are of good quality. You're better off spending your money on two good knives rather than lots of cheap knives. Keep them sharp, handwash them, and they'll last for years.

organic food for less

389 JOIN A CLUB

For organic food, buying clubs are a great idea. If there isn't one in your area, think about setting one up. The more members you have, the cheaper things are.

389 DO SOME RESEARCH

The best way to buy organic food without paying a premium is to do some research. Ask around at local stores and phone your local food advice service to see where the best bargains are to be had.

390 BUY SOME SHARES

Have a look in your local area to see if there are any community-supported local growing programmes. Usually you can buy a share in them, which will help provide you with seasonal food for at least some of the year and it's a great way to get good food for less.

391 BOX IT UP

A great way to get organic vegetables on the cheap is to invest in an organic box from a local producer or national organic scheme. The best way to do this is to buy as much as you can and try to share it with a neighbour or group if friends. You'll need to be prepared to be creative with your cooking though, as you won't always know what to expect.

392 GO TO MARKET

Farmers' markets are great for fresh produce. They are often cheaper than stores because they cut out the middleman. Look for seasonal bargains and haggle on price for bulk buying. Go near closing time and offer to buy their remaining stock for a low price.

393 GROW YOUR OWN

By far the best way to get cheap organic produce is to grow your own. You don't even need a lot of space. Summer fruit like strawberries and tomatoes can be grown in small pots, as can herbs. You won't get fresher than home-grown either.

reuse & recycle

395 TAKE A SHOWER

Next time you're staying in a hotel, take the shower cap. It's great for wrapping around shoes in suitcases to protect the rest of the packed items and will stop you having to buy shoe covers. Or use old socks instead.

396 A NICE CUP OF TEA

Don't throw away your old tea bags or the dregs from the teapot – use them as fertilizer for pot plants and your plants will soon be lush and green. Not only is this a great way of avoiding waste, it will stop you having to buy expensive products.

397 TIGHTEN UP

Old tights (panty hose) are great for storing flower bulbs and onions in the garage or shed, as they keep them off the ground and away from moisture that might ruin them. A very different way of reusing them is to scrunch them up and use them to plump up old cushions (pillows) that have gone 'flat'.

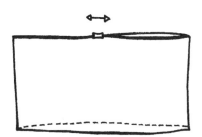

398 WASH AND REUSE

Rather than throwing away press-close sandwich bags or Ziploc storage bags, rinse them out and reuse them. The ones with the plastic tabs are made from different types of plastic so are rarely recycled. In addition to using them for food storage, they can be used for kid's toys, such as Legos or felt-tip markers, or to store the cords and accessories that come with electronic items, such as cameras, MP3 players and computers. By cutting a small hole in one corner, a bag will also make an excellent icing bag for frosting cakes.

399 SOCK THE DOG

If you have a dog, don't spend lots of money on toys that he/she will only destroy. Stuff a used tennis ball down an old, long sock and tie a knot in the sock to keep the ball in place. Your dog will have hours of fun! Also, when your towels are becoming a little worn, don't just throw them away, use them to dry off the dog after walks in the rain, as sleeping mats in the house, or for the dog to sit on in the car.

400 GET A REFILL

You can buy refills for some eco-friendly house-cleaning products that reduce your waste and cost because you're not buying the packaging that usually goes with it.

401 BE A JAR LOVER

Don't throw away screw-top jars. The airtight lid makes them great for storing snacks, cookies and other dry goods, or use them in the garage to help keep screws, bolts etc., safe and organized.

402 SAVE YOUR PLASTIC

Don't throw away the plastic cutlery you get with fast food or pre-packed foods. Knives, forks and even the teaspoons you get with coffee can be great for picnics or parties, saving you the cost of having to buy them.

403 REUSE YOUR BAGS

If you still use the plastic bags from the supermarket, don't throw them away when you unpack your groceries. Reuse them when you next go shopping (often, the supermarket will give you a discount for doing this) or use them for bin liners (trash bags).

404 CUSHION THE BLOW

Use up old material by making cushions (pillows). All you need is two squares of material the same size and some stuffing material (either buy it cheap or use old clothes or rags). Put the right sides of the material together, sew along three sides, turn the right way out, stuff and sew the hem. Simple!

405 CUT UP A CARTON

If your milk and fruit juice comes in clear containers, or you use bottled water, you can use the containers in the garden once you've finished with them. Cut off the top of the bottle and upend it over tender plants and stems to protect them.

406 SAVE YOUR TUBS

Empty margarine tubs make great single- or double-portion freezing tubs for your leftover meals. Wash and dry them, then store for use next time you need to put a serving's worth of pasta sauce or some other leftover meal in the freezer.

407 PACKAGE IT UP

Save all the wrapping that comes your way, such as bubble wrap, tissue and other packaging. Use it to send presents or things you have sold on the Internet – you'll make less money out of selling your stuff if you have to pay out for packaging materials.

cleaning up

408 DAB AWAY FINGERS

Don't repaint finger-marked walls, simply use a piece of bread to dab away the finger marks. The bread should be soft and white for best results, and don't eat it afterwards!

408 REDUCE YOUR AMOUNTS

Try snapping dishwasher or laundry tablets in half and see if they do as good a job. Use one squirt of oven cleaner instead of two. Because the manufacturer sets the amounts, they may well recommend that you use more than you really need to, so it's worth experimenting.

410 BUY THE SODA

Bicarbonate of soda (baking soda) is a great deodorizer and stain remover. Use it to clean the inside of the fridge and microwave and to remove nasty smells from the fridge and cupboards. You can even use it to descale teapots and mugs and remove tea stains.

411 CLEANING BRUSH

Don't throw away your old toothbrush – relegate it to be used for cleaning or shoe polishing. It's great for getting into hard-to-reach areas, and because it's been used the bristles will be soft and won't scratch. Cleaning the grout between tiles is another great toothbrush job!

412 JUICY POLISH

Make your own cheap furniture polish using olive oil and a drop of lemon juice. Use it to get rid of cup and mug rings on wooden tables and to buff up leather and polish wood.

413 GET HALF CLEAN

Cleaning products, such as kitchen paper towels, dusters, washing cloths and sponges, can be expensive, so try cutting them in half to double their value. You can also try this with tumble-dryer sheets and facial wipes.

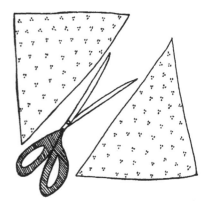

414 GET A SHOE RACK

Carpets that people walk on in shoes don't last as long. Make it a rule that everyone takes off their outdoor shoes before they come in, and if necessary get a shoe rack in your hall.

415 VALUE OF VINEGAR

Don't use expensive mould cleaner – simply wipe cupboards and bread bins (boxes) with a vinegar-soaked cloth. It will help keep mould away for good. Use vinegar and screwed-up newspaper to clean windows for a cheap, professional shine. You can also use white wine vinegar instead of expensive shower cleaner – wipe it on, leave to soak for a few minutes if the shower is grimy, then rinse well and polish dry.

416 STORE THE POWDER

Always have some cheap laundry detergent powder to hand for cleaning in the kitchen. Boil it up in burnt pans to make them sparkle, and you can also use it for effective degreasing and stain removal.

417 CLEAN WITH COLA

If you've got cola left over from a party or dinner, or simply in the fridge, throw a little down the toilets and around the sinks and leave them overnight. They'll come up sparkling (and it might make you think twice before spending your well-earned cash on drinking it again!).

418 SOAK YOUR SOCKS

Instead of throwing your socks away when they become smelly or drowning them in laundry detergent, soak them in a mixture of five parts water to one part vinegar – it will cut through the smell and grime in no time.

419 WATER IT DOWN

We all know how retailers use water to help make their goods last longer, but did you know that you can use it to eke out savings at home as well? Washing-up (dishwashing) liquid, shampoo, milk, yeast extract and a lots of other items can be watered down, with little effect on to their taste, performance, etc.

420 OPEN THE WINDOW

Air fresheners are an expensive way to fragrance your home, and most of them don't actually 'freshen' the air. Why not dispense with them altogether and open a window or door instead? Fresh air is the best air freshener, and it's free!

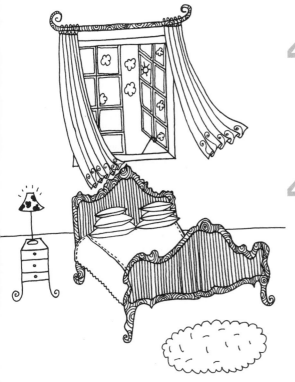

421 CHEAP CLEAN

Chances are the cleaning products in your household grocery costs make up a large part of the expense. However, you don't always need expensive cleaners as you can do pretty much everything with vinegar, bicarbonate of soda (baking soda) and washing-up (dishwashing) liquid. Add a few drops of essential oil if you want it to smell fresh.

422 DON'T FAN IT

Instead of turning on your extractor fan, which uses a lot of expensive electricity, get rid of cooking smells by simply putting a saucer of vinegar by the cooker (stove). The vinegar absorbs the smells and leaves your kitchen odour-free.

423 USE MICROFIBRE

For dusting, try using a microfibre cloth instead of spending money on polish. Not only will it save you money on products, it will also save you time on dusting because it actually picks up the dust rather than spreading it around the room. You can often buy them cheap in discount stores.

424 DESCALE THE KETTLE

You don't need to buy specialist products to descale your kettle, just boil up a mixture of half vinegar and half water and leave it overnight. Put this half-and-half solution in a pump dispenser and use it to clean bathroom tiles and Thermos flasks, and as a fabric softener, window cleaner and air freshener (in a pump dispenser).

425 POWER OF SOAP

Don't underestimate the power of hot soapy water to get things really clean. Make the water as hot as you can, add some washing-up (dishwashing) liquid and leave the item to soak for half an hour before you clean it. You'll get sparkling results.

426 BE AN UNBLOCKER

Don't pay a plumber to unblock your sink, try to do it yourself first. Throw a handful of bicarbonate of soda (baking soda) and a cup of vinegar down the sink, wait a couple of hours and pour on a kettle of boiling water to see if the blockage lifts.

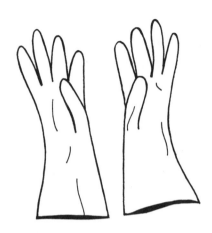

427 BAND IT

Don't throw away your dishwashing gloves when you've finished with them. You can turn the fingers into finger guards and make elastic bands from the palm part of the glove.

428 IRON THE IRON

Irons usually last for several years, but you can make yours last even longer by looking after it. Taking care, rub soap on a hot iron plate and then wipe it off when it has cooled, get a waxy iron cleaning stick and descale your iron regularly.

429 BLEACH AWAY STAINS

If you have blood or other dark stains on white sheets, you can bleach it off using a paste of talcum powder and bleach. Rub it in then allow to dry enough so that you can vacuum it away. The stain should disappear.

430 CLEAN THE OVEN

To clean your oven, wait until it's cooled down, but still warm, and wipe it over with a vinegar-soaked cloth. Not only will this clean your oven, it will also prevent it smelling. For really grimy ovens 'bake' a pot of boiling water containing lemon juice in it for a few hours, then turn it off. As soon as it's cool enough to touch, wipe over with the rest of the water mixed with bicarbonate of soda (baking soda) and vinegar.

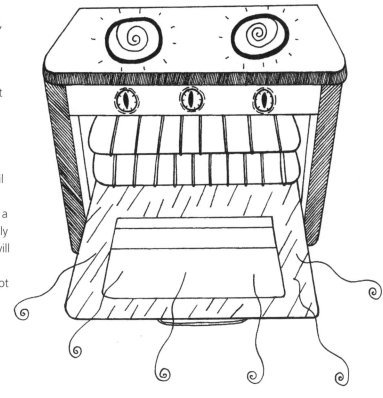

home improvements

431 DOUBLE UP

If you don't have double glazing, use plastic sheeting over windows to cut heating costs in winter or make your own frame to go over the window from wood and glass to create a winter glazing panel.

432 GIVE TILES A LICK

Instead of replacing the tiles in your bathroom, for a quick and cheap update use tile paint instead. Tiles can be really expensive and if you just want to change the colour then paint may be a cheaper option.

433 STUFF THE GAP

Instead of getting new windows, which can be a massive expense, stave off winter draughts by using cling film (plastic wrap). Simply stuff cling film (plastic wrap) into the window gaps for an (almost) invisible and totally draught-free solution.

434 ACT RICH

To help you get that 'wealthy' feeling, pay attention to all the ways poverty has crept into your home. It isn't expensive to mend a lamp, take the stains out of the carpet or oil creaking doors, but it helps you live in comfort, ease and beauty, which makes you feel wealthier.

435 PRISTINE BRUSHES

Prevent your paintbrushes from going dry while you have a break between coats, by wrapping a plastic bag around the head. The same method can be used for rollers. They can be left for around 24 hours if the bag is airtight, but make sure you wash out well when you're finished with them otherwise you won't be able to use them again.

436 BUY EXTRA PAPER

If you are buying a wallpaper that might go out of stock, always buy some extra. If you have to replace a section at a later date because of damage, damp or building work, you want to be sure that you can match it up to avoid having to replace the whole lot.

437 BE CONFIDENT

When it comes to jobs around the house, only take on things you're confident with. Paying someone to redo a botched job is almost always more expensive than getting them to do it in the first place, so make sure you can finish what you start.

438 ODD-JOB BOX

If you do repairs and maintenance around the house it's worth keeping an odd-job box for screws and other accessories so you won't have to buy new every time. Keeping them in one place makes you less likely to replace them needlessly. You can benefit from bulk buying too.

439 BORROW TOOLS

Instead of accumulating a veritable showcase of power tools that you only use once a year, why not borrow from neighbours? You can even coordinate your buying with them to pool resources and prevent having to spend more money.

440 WORK FAST

Getting to work on small household jobs, like dripping taps (faucets) and flaking wallpaper, sooner rather than later is a good money-saving move. Minor problems are often quick and easy to solve and you can do them yourself, whereas if you leave them until crisis point you're far more likely to have to call in (and pay) a professional.

441 BE A BIN HUNTER

Check out the bargain bin at do-it-yourself stores where people have ordered paint colours and not picked them up. Think creatively – you might not want bright red, for instance, but mixing it with a yellow tester pot and that old tin of white in the shed could give you a light orange to go with the wallpaper you've chosen for the hall. Do a test first to check the dry colour before painting a whole wall or room.

442 OIL THOSE HINGES

The best way to stop expensive problems with doors, windows and furniture is to keep them well serviced. Use WD-40 (or a similar product) on hinges and candle wax on drawer runners to keep everything working smoothly.

443 POWDER AWAY CREAKS

Instead of calling in a carpenter the minute your stairs or floorboards become creaky, try an almost free home-improvement tip: sprinkle talcum powder between the cracks and see if that solves the problem.

444 RULE OF ONE

You don't have to spend lots of money painting a whole room to change the look. Simply change the colour of one 'signature' wall can give it a whole new lease of life for a far lower cost.

electrical goods

445 CALL THE MANUFACTURER

If you have a problem with an appliance call the manufacturer's customer care line. Even if your product isn't under warranty they might be able to help you with common problems and issues, replacement parts and so on.

446 ONLINE SOLUTIONS

Before you take the plunge and call in the professionals, take a look online to see if other people have had the same problem with an appliance and see what their solution was. You can often find handy tips for solving problems yourself and advice on when to repair and when to give in and replace it.

447 TIME YOUR PROGRAMMES

If you have cheap electricity at night, time your appliance programmes so they use electricity during this time. If they haven't got built-in timers, you can buy timers to fit onto the wall socket that serve the same purpose.

448 CLEAN YOUR COILS

Cleaning the coils at the back of your fridge will help it continue to function effectively, which will help keep your electricity costs as low as possible. Fridges are a big drain on power, so make sure the door seals are working properly so that you are not wasting energy unnecessarily.

449 HANG THEM OUT

Tumble dryers are big energy consumers. Hanging clothes on a washing line or drying rack is free. Alternatively, make a ceiling hanger from coat hangers and wooden dowels to hang clothes inside.

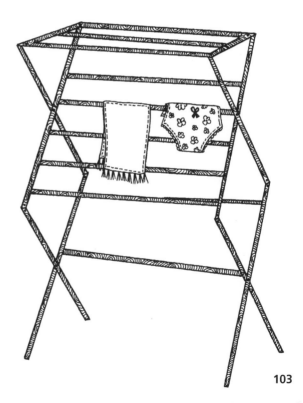

450 READ THE INSTRUCTIONS

It might sound simple, but before you call an engineer to fix your appliance, make sure you read the instructions. Often they have troubleshooting sections that may help you fix the problem on your own. Keep all your instruction manuals in one place for easy reference.

451 GET LEVEL

Appliances are tried, tested and function best when they are on a level surface, so get the spirit level out. Adjust the feet if necessary and make sure you're giving them the best chance to perform effectively.

452 EMPTY AND FULL

Your electrical appliances (dishwasher, washing machine, tumble dryer, vacuum cleaner, and so on) will all work best if you keep them 'empty' and 'full'. To explain what seems contradictory advice, this means topping up with products like rinse aid, emptying bags or compartments, and cleaning filters regularly to keep your appliances working optimally.

453 FILL YOUR FREEZER

A full freezer is actually cheaper to run than a half-full one as the food, once frozen, keeps itself cold. Keep it organized and tidy so you can minimize time with the door open. Try to keep food together and fill empty spaces with plastic containers of water or bags of ice cubes.

454 SCRAPE YOUR PLATES

Your dishwasher will struggle to perform optimally if you don't scrape (and even rinse) plates, bowls and cutlery before you put them in. Blocking the pipes and filters with excess food will only make it work harder, costing you money and leaving your dishes less than sparkling clean.

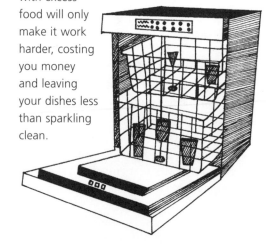

455 BAG A BAG SEALER

A bag sealer is a great money-saving appliance, as it will help keep foods airtight in cupboards and the freezer, which reduces waste. They can be picked up cheaply and you will quickly wonder how you ever managed without one.

furniture & soft furnishings

456 WINDOW DRESSING

Curtains can be a really expensive addition to your house, so getting them on the cheap is a great idea. Making curtains and decorative tie-backs yourself with material sourced from discount stores or the Internet is the best option, or scour charity (thrift) stores for curtains that you can alter to fit your windows.

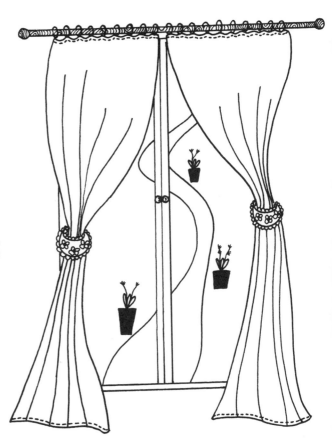

457 FIND A FOCUS

The best way to style a room on a budget is to find a focal point and work your look around it – bargain finds are great, but unless the look is pulled together they might look like exactly what they are! Create a 'look' using your favourite items or colours and work everything around it. Take photos and samples with you when you go bargain hunting to ensure that you buy coordinating items.

458 PATCHED TOGETHER

If you can't afford to buy a rug you can make your own using carpet sample squares that you can buy cheaply or even take for free from a local store. Simply patch the squares together and use gaffer (duct) tape to secure them underneath. Alternatively, make a rag rug by crocheting long strips of fabric together and stitching them in a coil.

459 MAKE YOUR OWN ART

Instead of buying expensive art for your walls, make your own modern art using cheap frames and leftover wallpaper. Simply frame pieces of the paper and arrange artfully for a thoroughly stylish, cheap decoration.

460 A BID FOR LUXURY

Housing auctions are great places to pick up quality furniture at a low price. You can often find real bargains, but be aware that you will usually have to pick up the items soon after you've bought them so make sure you've got room for them before you bid.

461 STAPLE IT IN

Reupholstering furniture needn't be an expensive job – all you need is a staple gun and some discount material or cheap leftovers from a local store. Cover the seat pad or back and staple it in place. If you want to give it a total overhaul you can cover seams with decorative trim or ribbon.

462 GIVE IT A FRESHEN UP

Second-hand furniture is a great way to furnish your home cheaply, but don't be afraid to give it a makeover. Apply a coat of fresh paint, change the handles for something modern (or funky for kids' rooms), create a stencilled design or sand it for a distressed look and it will look like designerware for a fraction of the cost.

463 CALL IT IN

Don't worry if you can't get to an auction in person, you can still pick up bargains by phone or by placing an absent bid. You state your highest amount and an auction worker bids for you. It's a good way to bid on items you would otherwise miss.

464 INVEST YOUR TIME

The best places to source stylish, but inexpensive, finds for your home are car-boot (garage) sales, markets and auctions. You're bound to find quality goods for a steal that would grace any home, but be prepared to search through nine things you hate for every good one.

465 FOCUS ON WALLS

Wallpaper can be expensive, but you don't need to do the whole room – a neat styling idea is to paper just one wall, a chimney breast or alcove. You can even use a single strip down one of the walls. You can accent this further by hanging pictures on the rest of the wall, or even only on the wallpapered section.

466 ADD A FINAL TOUCH

Finishing touches are worth their weight in gold when it comes to budget home furnishing. Simple craft projects, like making cushions (pillows), sewing tassels on sofas or blankets and adding some scented candles, can all help make a room look complete.

building works

467 KEEP THE JUNK

If you're having building work done don't let the builder take away tiles and other building materials without getting your share of the profit. Either ask them to leave them and sell them yourself or agree to share any money he/she makes (usually a better option, as they will have contacts to sell to).

468 GO MILITARY

It's worth browsing around an army surplus store if you are on the hunt for tools. Ex-military tools are usually of really good quality as they are made to last, and they're often very cheap.

469 GET ADJUSTABLE

An adjustable spanner (wrench) is a great budget buy as it allows you to secure a whole range of different bolt sizes. Be careful to use it correctly and if you're using cheap bolts, protect the bolt head from damage with a soft cloth.

470 DIY CONSTRUCTION

If you are a keen DIY enthusiast and on a limited budget, consider adding to the value of your home by constructing decking, a patio, a garage or garden shed, or a conservatory (sunroom). There are many manufactures of DIY kits on the market that have back-up online and helpline advice for installation.

471 WORK IN PART

Just because you can't do all of a job, doesn't mean you can't do any of it. You might not be able to build the wall, but you could dig trenches, clear out furniture and unpick roof tiles to cut building costs.

472 PLAN ON BUSTING YOUR BUDGET

Whenever you are having building work done, make sure you add between 10–15 per cent to the overall budget as a contingency. This will allow you to keep your cash flow going when (and it is when, not if) your work goes over budget and will prevent you having to borrow, which is expensive.

473 SHOP AROUND

Don't assume all the materials your builder uses have to be new. Shop around salvage yards (or get your builders to do it for you if you trust them) for reclaimed tiles, bricks and stone, which can often be cheaper than new, and certainly have more character.

474 THREE-QUOTE RULE

Always get at least three quotes for building work before you get anything done, and if possible use builders recommended by friends and neighbours. Don't automatically choose the cheapest – look for the best value and a good, thorough job that's built to last.

475 THINK AHEAD

The key to any building job is to plan ahead. Think about what you want from the job, what your priorities are and how strict your budget is. Stay on top of it while it's happening and communicate with your builders – make sure they know what your key aims are and what you expect of them.

476 TIME IT RIGHT

Make sure you get a written start and end date from your builder and make sure they understand that you will link it to payment. Some builders will accept a reduced rate if they run over. Another option is to set pay dates around how much of the job is done.

477 HOLD SOMETHING BACK

It's prudent, however much you trust your builder, to hold back some of the end fee (2–5 per cent) for a few weeks or months until they've finished all the 'snagging' – little jobs that are left over at the end of building work. Make sure you check the finished work thoroughly – look for missing tiles, chips, scratches and other details – before making the final payment.

478 THE IMPORTANCE OF INSURANCE

If you're building your own house make sure you get insurance to protect against theft, vandalism and also accidents. You don't want to be stung with medical bills if someone has an accident on your site during the build.

buying & selling

479 USE YOUR IMAGINATION

Instead of looking at the seller's furniture in the house you're looking over, imagine how your furniture and lifestyle would fit into it. Can you see yourself relaxing on your sofa in the lounge? Is the kitchen somewhere you could work? Does the bedroom feel appealing?

480 MAKE IT GOOD

If you want to maximize the possibility of selling your house, make sure it is clean and bright and that all of the little jobs are done before people look around. Flaking wallpaper, unpainted patches of wall and dirty floors are all big turnoffs for buyers.

481 SELL A MOOD

It's not just your house you're trying to sell, it's a lifestyle. The smell of fresh coffee, vases of flowers and magazines on a table are all ways to make your house more alluring and help buyers to see themselves relaxing there.

482 THE RIGHT APPROACH

When it comes to houses, first impressions count. If you're trying to sell, make sure the front of your house looks good as it will be the first thing prospective buyers see and they are likely to make judgements about the rest of the property based on it. Make sure the lawn is cut, lights work, paintwork is tidy and driveway is weed free.

483 LOOK DEEPER

When you're looking round a house don't be swayed by the efforts the owners will have made to help you feel at home. Ignore fires, coffee, bread smells and other 'dressing' and really look at the house. Do the walls look secure? Will you be able to heat it efficiently? How much structural work needs doing?

484 COUNT YOUR CASH

Before you decide to buy, make sure you've got enough cash not only for the house itself, but for furniture, soft furnishings and other expenses, such as a solicitor (attorney), taxes and surveys. It's important to budget carefully as moving house can be an extremely expensive business.

485 GET A LEGAL RECOMMENDATION

For your house move try to use a solicitor (attorney) who has been recommended to you. Ask friends and acquaintances who have moved recently and try to get the best you can. You can save money on legal fees in the long run by not skimping on the quality of professional you choose.

486 VISIT MORE THAN ONCE

Visit a house more than once before you decide to buy. Visit at different times of the day to see how the atmosphere changes and how it would fit your lifestyle and budgets. That quiet location might be great in the daytime, but would it be safe at night? Would your money-saving vegetables grow in that north-facing garden?

487 GET ADVICE

Get mortgage advice before you visit (real) estate agents. Knowing your options and likely market charges beforehand can stop you losing money by falling for one of their inhouse deals. Shop around so that you're knowledgeable and you'll get a better deal.

488 COMPILE A CHECKLIST

When you are thinking about moving house, make a checklist to take with you to viewings so that you don't lose sight of your priorities or your budgets. If you're viewing lots of houses they can tend to blur into one, so asking questions and taking notes on priorities is a great idea.

outdoor space

489 START FROM SEED

One packet of tomato seeds is often equivalent to the price of one tomato seedling plant, yet you get the potential of at least 30–40 plants in each packet. While it requires planning and takes longer, starting from seed can reap big savings. Use recycled containers like yogurt pots and a 'stolen' heat source such as the top of the microwave or water heater.

490 BE A COMPOSTER

Not only is having a compost heap the greener option, it will reduce the cost of having garden waste taken away or transporting it yourself to the dump, plus you'll have free (and chemical-free) fertilizer. In addition, the natural properties of compost help stop the spread of disease, which means costly measures are less likely. You can put anything on it, from grass and wood to coffee grounds, natural fibre clothing and fruit and vegetable peelings.

491 PLAN AHEAD

Make a list of what you'd really like to see in your garden and stick to it. A list will keep you under control when you see the end-of-season sales and are tempted to purchase something on a whim. In addition, if you plan exactly where plants are going to go, you won't make expensive last-minute mistakes, such as placing sun-loving plants in the shade.

492 GROW YOUR OWN

Growing your own vegetables is definitely a super-sized money saver, but it does take some work. Start with easy plants like beans and tomatoes and work your way into it slowly to avoid getting overwhelmed.

493 MULTIPURPOSE PLANTS

Wherever you can, try to choose plants that add to your garden in more than one way. For example, choose those that attract beneficial insects, like fennel, coriander (cilantro) and borage, or ones that are evergreen so you have colour all year round. Alternatively, plant trees that will bear fruit or give shade in summer.

494 WASH AWAY WEEDS

Instead of buying expensive (and potentially damaging) chemicals, you can easily make your own weedkiller with a cup of vinegar and half a cup of washing-up (dishwashing) liquid or even white vinegar straight from the bottle. Alternatively, pour on boiling water, then pull them up.

495 GET FREE WOOD

Talk to your local farm or forestry service to see if you can take wood for fires and garden use for free, or at a low price rather than paying a premium. Woodworking stores often have left over wood that they are pleased to get rid of cheaply or for free if you pick it up.

496 DO A SEED SWAP

Why not save your seeds in the growing season and arrange a swap with some friends or neighbours? You will boost the variety of plants in your garden without spending any cash and the varieties will be tried and tested. Because soil conditions are usually the same, doing this within a local radius is best.

497 USE CLIMBERS

A climbing variety is usually a better budget choice than the same plant in a bush variety because it will produce more crop for a longer time and leave you more space for growing other plants.

498 GARDENING BUDDY

A gardening buddy is not only a good move for helping you to be a better gardener, as you can exchange ideas and information with them, it's also a great money-saving move as you can share the cost. Buy one packet of seeds between two, for instance, share gardening tools or benefit from bulk buying.

499 JOIN A CLUB

Joining a gardening club is a great way to save yourself money. In addition to helping to keep your enthusiasm going by allowing you to mix with other gardeners, they also usually run sharing schemes for cuttings, seeds and plants, and members often also get good discounts at local garden centres.

fashion purchases

500 MAKE IT YOUR AIM

Look at what you spend over the course of a year on clothes. Then make it your job the following year to buy everything for half the price. Even if you give yourself a small gift for reaching your goal, you're still going to be in credit.

501 DON'T ASK DON'T GET

Don't be shy about asking for discounts, even in major retail stores. Most of the time stores are so keen to make a sale that they will find some leeway to lower the price.

502 THINK VERSATILE

Most women wear 20 per cent of their clothing 80 per cent of the time. Wherever you can, buy versatile clothing that can be used with more than one outfit – for example, black trousers or jeans can be worn with different jackets and tops or shirts. Try to only buy clothes that will go with what you already have.

503 ARE YOU SURE?

If you buy something that you aren't sure about when you get it home, take it back! Don't wait to see if it will grow on you, it will sit in the back of your wardrobe wasting money. Never be afraid to return an item if you change your mind about it.

504 THINK BEFORE YOU BUY

Unless you've got a specific event like a wedding or an important party, make it a rule never to buy a whole outfit in one go. That way, you'll teach yourself to think about the rest of your wardrobe every time you shop, rather than buying lots of different items that you won't use.

505 ORPHAN OR FRIEND?

Sometimes, we'd all love to buy that cheeky designer dress or exquisite silk beaded blouse, but will you actually wear it? Before you waste money on luxury items, ask yourself if it will have friends in your wardrobe, and a place in your lifestyle. Don't buy 'orphan' pieces that will sit alone on a hanger for years.

506 SUIT SEPARATES

If you're buying a suit from a department store, take advantage of separates. Jackets always last longer than skirts or trousers, so try and buy two bottoms for each top to avoid having to get rid of a perfectly good jacket later.

507 LAYER UP

Instead of buying separate clothes for winter and summer, try to develop the type of wardrobe that you can layer – layering up in the winter and down in the summer – and buy items that you can use for all-season wear, Anyway, layering up is warmer than a single, thick layer.

508 MAKE IT MATCH

Before you buy an item of clothing, think practically about when and where you will wear it and what other items of clothing you have to go with it. Take a picture (mental or otherwise) of your wardrobe with you when you go shopping so you can be sure you're buying something that fits your look, not just because the particular item suits you.

509 AVOID CREDIT

Store cards are among the worst interest rates of all, so if you are buying clothes stick to a simple rule – only buy what you can afford to pay for at the end of the month. If you are going to need to pay interest to have the item, don't buy it. Save up until you have the cash.

510 FIGHT THE FRENZY

Shopping in discount stores is a great way to save money, but only if you stick to buying what you went in there for. If you load up with cheap items, just because they're cheap, it defeats the object of going in the first place. Don't get in a 'cheap' frenzy and buy more than you need.

511 GO ONLINE

Once you've found a brand you like, check online before you buy. Trying on your favourite jeans and then buying them on eBay or other online retail outlets could save you a significant amount, so make sure you do your research before you buy.

512 KEEP A JOURNAL

At the beginning of each season, go through your wardrobe and write down the things that you think you need to buy new – check them off the list as you buy them and add anything new. That way, you can keep the list in mind if bargains come up and you'll avoid wasting money on items you don't need.

513 WRITE IT DOWN

Work out if you're shopping well or wasting your money by keeping a note of where and when you buy clothes, how much you wear them, and when and why you get rid of them. After doing this for a year, or even a few months, you might start to find a pattern emerging that will help you maximize your money.

514 GO ELECTRONIC

Sign up for e-mail newsletters from retailers, and they'll send you coupons and keep you informed about their latest sales. There are entire websites devoted to mining the net for coupons, but searching through them can be time consuming. Instead, choose your favourite stores and sign up for individual updates.

515 FIND A FACTORY

If you like a particular brand of clothing, you can save up to 50 per cent by shopping at factory outlet stores. The best thing to do is contact the brand itself to find out where they send factory seconds and excess stock.

516 BE SENSIBLE

Look carefully at the trends and try to separate them into two – key pieces that will last several years and seasonal items that will be over by next season, let alone next year. Make sure you spend the majority of your money (say, 80 per cent) on key pieces and save the rest for trends.

517 HIRE A CONSULTANT

Even though it might seem an unnecessary expense, hiring a fashion consultant can be a great way to save money. The right person should be able to save you money by helping you make sure all your clothing is working together effectively.

518 BE PATIENT

Even though you may want that item immediately, ask yourself if you really need it. Make it a rule to only buy things you really need straightaway – for others create a wish list and wait until the price comes down by 20, 30 or 50 per cent (whichever suits you best). Develop a habit of watching the stores so you can buy when the items are reduced.

519 LABELS FOR LESS

Get couture clothing, bags, shoes and accessories for less by shopping at designer clearance sales, sample racks (if you are conveniently model size), preview sales and online at websites like www.dress-for-less.com. Also look at the 'rag trade' area of any big city where you will find the wholesaler shops and cutting rooms that may run open-to-the-public sales.

520 BUY TO LAST

When you are buying clothes, try to purchase durable products, even if they are a little more expensive. Well-made clothes have heavy seams and added reinforcement at stress points to ensure the product survives daily use. Avoid items with flimsy seams or fabric that won't wash well.

521 CHOOSE CLASSICS

Instead of going for clothes in the season's latest colour, choose basics in classic styles and neutral shades that will last more than one season and simply add fashionable accessories – like an inexpensive scarf or bag – to make it seem more current.

522 KEEP IT IN THE FAMILY

When you're building a budget wardrobe, it pays to think in colour families. If your entire range of clothes is black and grey, for example, don't buy lots of navy, even if it's a hot trend. Keep your current clothing in mind when you shop, and don't buy anything that won't go with at least two or three other items that you own.

523 SOLO SHOP

When it comes to shopping, if you've done your preparation and research and you know what you need, it's best to go alone. That way, you won't be persuaded to buy things you don't really need or that don't fit your purpose. If you're out with friends, arrange to have a 'single' half-hour where you can really go and concentrate, then meet up again later.

524 GET WOOLLY

Chain stores are great, but the reason they're great is because their clothes are cheap. In most cases, you can get away with it, but often their knitwear is where they fall down. Try to purchase knitwear with high wool counts to avoid that bobbly, washed look.

525 BUY OFF-SEASON

For new clothes, think about buying your clothes off-season when they are on sale. Stock up on commonly worn all-year-round items like T-shirts, shirts, underwear and jeans when they are discounted.

526 PAIR THEM UP

Don't skimp on standards like jeans, black trousers and good shoes. A classic, crisp white cotton blouse is another great investment as it can be dressed up or down and will got with almost anything. When fit and style is of the utmost importance, a cheap imitation just won't do, so buy the very best your budget will allow. By searching out some cheaper trendy, unusual and/or colourful pieces to wear with your good quality items, you can get a fashionable twist without looking cheap and tacky.

527 A PATIENT SHOPPER

By waiting just a few months to pick up the latest fashions, you'll get more for your money. For example, autumn/winter clothes typically hit the racks in midsummer and start getting marked down a couple of months later. If you can wait, even a little longer than this, to buy then you can save up to a massive 75 per cent (plus, you'll be buying the clothes is when you actually need to wear them!).

second-hand & vintage

528 A GIRL'S BEST FRIEND

If you are hunting for serious antique jewellery or real gemstones, such as diamonds, you need to research well. Know the time period, jewellery house and carat size you are looking for, as well as your metals. Get to know your precious metal hallmarks to make sure you're getting exactly what you are paying for.

529 THINK AHEAD

One of the best ways to waste money on expensive clothing is to leave it until the last minute to think about the party outfit you need to buy. Visit charity (thrift) stores regularly to keep an eye on what they have in stock. You won't be able to walk in and find the perfect little black dress on the day you need it, but you might find the perfect outfit on another visit and keep it to wear on the right occasion.

530 CHEAP AND CHEERFUL

Vintage reproduction jewellery pieces can be fun, quirky and rock-bottom cheap. Consider beads, fake pearls and zircon for inexpensive dressing-up fun, but above all buy what you really love – anything bought on a whim that you won't actually wear is an expensive mistake.

531 LOOK FOR WEIGHT AND BRIGHTNESS

If jewellery looks worn, chipped or dingy or has had obvious repairs, it won't have such a high value. Pieces that are of substantial weight, have pronged settings and smooth, bright stones will last longer and hold their value better.

532 GO GEOGRAPHIC

If you're looking for charity (thrift) store bargains check out stores in exclusive areas where the clothes are likely to be better quality, or those near big shopping centres or department stores as stores often donate unsold stock.

533 GONE BUT NOT FORGOTTEN

Good shopping spots for vintage labels are market stalls and shops in nursing homes and retirement villages. Often jewellery and garments are from the deceased and given by the family, who may not know the true value of what they are giving away. If you do your research you may find some hidden treasures that the seller isn't aware of.

534 HAVE A RUMMAGE

Once or twice a year, make a point of visiting a garage, church or jumble (rummage) sale to stock up on essentials like scarves and other key pieces. Choose colours that will complement your existing clothing.

535 BUY VINTAGE JEWELLERY NOT ANTIQUE

Whereas specialist vintage boutiques and antique fairs can be pricy, market stalls run by individuals with a passion for vintage items offer lower-priced pieces. This is especially true with costume jewellery. Although the offerings might not be of collector quality, they will still capture the character and beauty of a bygone age.

536 FABRIC FABULOUS

If you're shopping in charity (thrift) stores, don't just look for things in your size. Clothes in other sizes and men's clothes can often be easily altered to fit you or suit your style. Materials and fabrics are often good buys too.

selling & swapping

537 SHARE IT

A great idea for budget clothing is to swap clothes with your friends. Go round to each other's houses and look through wardrobes to see what would work for you. Agree to swap for a certain number of months, but remember to agree a policy beforehand that agrees what to do if an item is accidentally damaged or lost. Another idea is to hold a clothes swap party with similar-sized friends.

538 BRAND IT

If you're selling on eBay, brand names are really big news. Your 'cheap' bargain will sell, but if you've got real fashion brands you're more likely to make a killing. Consider 'bundling' clothes that go together to help boost the price.

539 BEST DEAL

If you live in a large city, there are likely to be a variety of dress agencies (consignment stores) in your area. Do some research before you visit – find out what they specialize in, what percentage of the sale price is yours to keep and whether there other fees involved, then choose the best deal for you.

540 BUFF IT UP

If you are selling clothes through a dress agency (consignment store), you'll get a better price for clothes that are clean, pressed and on hangers. The better the item looks, the more money it will make, so get out the shoe polish, the jewellery cleaner and scissors to cut any loose threads and maximize your money.

541 RUN A CLOTHING BUSINESS

Instead of letting clothing you don't wear anymore take up precious storage space, clean out your wardrobe at the end of every season. Sell any newish items you haven't worn on the Internet or at garage sales. Use the money you make to buy new clothes.

542 BUY AND RESELL

Making money out of dress agencies (consignment stores) doesn't have to be limited to what's in your own wardrobe. Search your local charity (thrift) stores for items you can sell to dress agencies (consignment stores) and you could make yourself a tidy profit to use to boost your own wardrobe.

543 BORROW IT

Many older relatives will have a pile of vintage clothing at the back of their wardrobes that they will never wear again. Not only could you get wear out of them, it might also give them pleasure to see you enjoying them, so ask if you can raid their wardrobe.

544 MAKE A FRIEND

Your local dress agency (consignment store) owner can be your best resource for making money out of clothes. She can tell you what merchandise is in demand, what shoppers are looking for and she may even be able to tell you what sizes, styles and brand names sell best. This information can be invaluable, especially if you're hunting the stores for items to resell.

mending & altering

545 GET HOOKED

One of the best investments you can make to keep your knitwear in tip-top condition is a steel crochet hook. Whenever you see a loose thread you can hook it inside to stop further fraying.

546 GET IT ALTERED

If you've found a whole lot of clothes in your wardrobe that don't fit you, don't throw them away. Take them to a clothes alteration service or alter them yourself if you can. This is especially true for clothing that is too large, which can almost always be easily made smaller.

547 DARN IT

Instead of leaving holes in socks until they are big and difficult to mend, make a point of repairing holes as soon as the tiniest one appears. That way, you're less likely to have to throw the sock away and it will take less material (and effort) to mend it.

548 ON THE MEND

Don't worry if you buy clothes in discount stores or sales that are slightly damaged. With a little effort you can mend most things at home. Problems that are difficult to solve and should be steered clear of are oil stains and long tears, as they are difficult to repair.

549 CREATE A COPY

Don't panic if your favourite wardrobe item is nearing the end of its life – while it's still wearable take the item to a seamstress and ask them to copy it. Better still, unpick the item and make a pattern so you can make your own version with a different fabric.

550 FIND A SEAMSTRESS

If you don't sew yourself, a seamstress or clothes-altering service could be your new best friend. Not only can they help you and your wardrobe cope with body changes like weight gain or loss and pregnancy, they can help turn inexpensive buys into bespoke items. Another idea is to swap skills with a friend who can sew.

551 GET SEWING

Even if you don't have the aptitude or attitude to learn how to tailor jeans or a skirt, learning how to make a few simple alterations can save you lots of money. Start by mastering the basics, like replacing buttons and hemming trousers, and you may soon find yourself inspired to try more elaborate projects.

DIY fashion

552 SEW IT UP

Many women's magazines carry free patterns so you'll only need to pay for materials, which you can buy from markets and discount material stores. Find a pattern that suits you and use it for several different items.

553 MAKE YOUR OWN JEWELLERY

You can make all types of jewellery at a fraction of the price with wire, elastic, beads and jewellery fasteners. Save your broken necklaces and bracelets, earrings that have lost their pair and ribbons or other small decorative elements you have around to make new pieces. Simply stringing a couple of large wooden beads onto a leather thong or ribbon can create an instant choker.

554 EMBROIDER AND EMBELLISH

If you are handy with needlework, you can lift an old fashion item, handbag or accessory with a little decorative embroidery. This is especially useful to hide stains or faults in the garment.

555 GET A PATTERN

If you know how to sew, but are scared of going 'off pattern', why not do a pattern-cutting course? They are usually inexpensive and if you could learn to 'copy' the latest trends and make them for yourself cheaply, think of the savings!

556 DYE IT, PRINT IT AND PAINT IT

Old T-shirts can be tie-dyed, painted with fabric paints or stamp-printed with motifs to create new clothes for almost no cost. Fabric marker pens can be used to outline fine details. These techniques work best on 100 per cent, tight-weave cotton.

557 ADD A RIBBON

Collect ribbons from giftboxes, boutique shopping bags and haberdashery shops or markets, and use them to give your existing clothes a new lease of life. Use the ribbons – or lace remnants or fringing – to replace shoulder straps on dresses and camisoles. Add wide ribbon as a border to the hem of dresses and skirts, or use it to edge a jacket. Simple sewing skills are all you'll need.

558 CUSTOMIZE WITH BEADS AND GEMS

Sew beads, sequins or gemstones on a dress or skirt to turn simple daywear into a special occasion outfit. If the garment has a floral or geometric pattern, embellish it along the lines of the design. Alternatively, stitch the beads along a neckline, cuffs or hemline.

559 BELT UP

Think imaginatively about ways to make belts from all kinds of fabrics and haberdashery items. Use a man's necktie, a scarf, or a woven or braided ribbon sewn to a d-ring or diamanté buckle. You may also like to attach rhinestones or studs to a cheap, simple mesh belt.

560 KNIT ONE PURL TWO

Create individual scarves, hats, tote bags, throws and jumpers (sweaters) by getting to work on knitting projects. There are many yarns available from wool and silk, to mohair and metallics, and they don't have to be expensive if you buy from discount shops.

561 PURSES AND TOTES

Look in thrift stores and charity shops for old placemats or table runners, that can be used to make durable handbags and totes. Sew two squares together or fold one rectangle over and stitch up the sides. Turn the top under and stitch it all the way around, leaving an opening to thread a drawstring through. Alternatively sew on bought handles.

recycle & reuse

562 WRAP IT UP

Make use of your old tights (panty hose) that you won't wear again. Wrap them around coat hangers to add padding, which will help protect your clothes.

563 SAVE THEM

If you have clothes that are damaged, or so old you can't donate them to a charity (thrift) store, keep them instead of throwing them away. They are great to use for packing up delicate items when you move house or if you are packing them up to store away.

564 COTTON HANDS

Make a pair of cotton hand mitts from an old shirt or T-shirt and wear them when you put on your tights (panty hose) or stockings to avoid snagging or causing a ladder (run). By doing this they'll last longer and you'll save money on having to buy replacements.

565 PROTECT YOUR CLOTHES

Instead of throwing away old T-shirts or work shirts, use them as protectors for your clothes in the wardrobe, to stop them rubbing against each other and causing damage.

566 SAVE YOUR BUTTONS

Never throw away a garment before removing and saving the buttons. They can be used for decorating or as replacements on other clothes, to augment charity-(thrift-) store bargains or even sold on to people who will use them.

caring for clothes

567 BE CAREFUL

Caring for your clothes is a great way to prolong their life and stop you having to buy new versions all the time. Keep office clothes looking good by changing as soon as you get home and wearing old clothing around the house.

568 KEEP WASHING LOW

One of the quickest ways to wear out clothes is to wash them all the time. Keep washing to a minimum, especially for outer garments that don't touch your skin. Using low temperatures whenever you can is not only better for the environment, but will also help your clothes stay newer looking.

569 WORK ON STAINS

Time is important, so act fast to stay stain-free. Make sure you always have a stash of stain removers in your home so you can work quickly to stop clothes being ruined beyond repair.

570 GET A VAC

A vac-bag is a great way to store clothes you're saving for another season as it keeps them in really good condition as well as giving you more space so you can see what's in your wardrobe. Vacuum bags prevent clothes being attacked by moths and reduces the chance of storage damage.

571 IN THE AIR

Hang clothes as soon as you take them off but to help preserve them, hang them in your bedroom or dressing room first before putting them in the wardrobe – that way they will get an airing before they are put away. If you don't have enough space, create multiple hangers for yourself by hanging three or four coat hangers on to each other so your clothes don't get crushed.

572 TURN IT OUT

Before you wash knitwear or brushed cotton in your washing machine, turn the item inside out. This helps prevent piling and bobbling of the material, which can make clothes look overworn.

573 PROTECT THE SEQUINS

If you have sequinned or beaded clothes, protect them in your wardrobe or chest of drawers using tissue paper from old store purchases. That way, you will avoid damaging them or other items and you'll have a use for all that unwanted paper!

574 GET WET

Dry-cleaning is expensive. If possible, try to buy clothes that don't need dry-cleaning then you will avoid the costs associated with it. Instead of dry-cleaning business suits, wash gently in the front-loading washing machine and iron with a plain tea towel between the iron and the item to prevent shiny marks appearing. Treating them gently and washing this way should be fine for all but the most delicate and expensive items.

clothing for children

575 LOCAL SALES

Often, local mothers' groups will run sales for children's clothes. Keep a look out for details of them in the local press, you may have to submit items in a certain way and before a certain date. Arrive early to bag bargains.

576 SHOP LARGE

Newborn babies grow so fast that there's little point buying lots of clothes for them as they'll only wear them for a few weeks. Instead, buy a few items and wash them regularly. Buy more clothes as they get bigger, as you will get more use out of them.

577 GET REINFORCED

Reinforce children's clothing in areas that get the most wear. Shoulders, buttons and other fastenings are all much-pulled-on areas, so it is worth putting a few extra stitches in to save major repairs later.

578 BORROW AND LEND

When it comes to children's clothes, borrowing, lending and swapping are great ways to save money as children grow out of their clothes so quickly. Ask friends and acquaintances whether they would be interested in working out an arrangement with you.

579 SHOP THE SALES

There is always a surfeit of children's clothes at garage sales and jumble (rummage) sales, but don't just look on the clothes hangers. People often put kids' clothes in buckets and baskets because they can't be bothered to iron them, so it's worth hunting around for a bargain.

580 MEASURE UP

Jot down your family's measurements and sizes in a small notebook or on a piece of paper that you can take with you when you go shopping. It may be useful to carry a tape measure with you as well, and then you be able to know if that bargain will definitely fit.

581 STORE AT HOME

If you're planning to have more children, once your children outgrow their clothes pack them away carefully into storage bins or bags and store them at home. If you are super-organized, you can sort them by gender so you know what you will be able to reuse at a glance.

582 MAKE SHORTS

Instead of buying new summer clothes for your child, turn the long, winter trousers that they've probably grown out of into shorts. If the waist and bottom still fits well, all you need is some iron-on webbing and you can create a new pair of shorts to last the summer.

583 BUY TO GROW

Children's clothing can be really frustrating and expensive to buy because they grow so quickly. Try to invest in clothes that can be altered as they get bigger. Trousers with adjustable waistbands and turn-ups (cuffs) that can be folded down and tops and jackets with arms that can be rolled up and down.

shoes

584 BE SENSIBLE

When it comes to shoes, sensible doesn't have to mean low heeled and boring, sensible means: will you wear them? If your lifestyle calls for lots of high heels then fine, but if you often wear boots or low heels, there's no justification – stick to what you use.

585 COBBLE IT TOGETHER

One of your best money-saving investments is a good shoe repairer. Being able to keep your shoes well heeled and mended is a great way to prolong their life and stop you having to buy more. Many shoe repairers also mend other leather goods, such as bags. As bags are a big expense for most women keeping them in good condition is a great money-saving tip.

586 TAKE A TIP

Keep a felt-tipped pen handy to cover scuffs you on the heels and rims of your shoes. Using a pen like this is a great way to hide marks and blemishes and to keep shoes looking newer for longer.

587 SHAPE OUT BOOTS

For most shoes the toe is the giveaway that they are getting older. With boots it's often the body of the boot that gets scrunched up in storage and starts to show its age. Invest in boot savers that will pad out the legs of your boots and keep them free from crinkles and creases.

588 PAPER TOE

If you have lots of shoes you don't wear that often, it helps to keep them in shape. Shoe shapers can be expensive so use newspaper to pad out the toe or keep the tissue pads from when you first bought them to keep shoes in shape even when your feet aren't in them.

589 GET COLOURFUL

The shoes that are most likely to have discounts on them in the sales, and are often marked down by a lot, are those in less 'safe' colours. Look for fun evening shoes or daytime flats in colours other than black and brown that will help complement your wardrobe.

590 CLASSIC OR TRENDY?

In every season there's a way to buy shoes that are classics, but that still look on-trend. The best bet is usually to go middle-of-the-road – try to find something that will go with many different outfits without appearing too in fashion. A classic mid-heel in the latest colour can be a good way to look up to the minute yet also buy to last.

591 DON'T BE TEMPTED

Remember that buying shoes you won't wear prevents you from buying those you really need, so don't waste your money on shoes that will sit in your wardrobe when a different style could be adorning your feet. Be honest with yourself.

592 SIGN UP

Sign up for newsletters, special offers and online deals at your favourite shoe stores. This way you will always get to know about upcoming sales before the rest of the general public, plus you are also likely to receive discount offers on shoes that aren't in the sale.

583 OFF-SEASON SHOES

The oldest trick in the book is to buy shoes at the end of a season, or even well into the next. Those shimmery sandals that are full price in the height of summer will be marked down substantially in just a few short months. The longer you wait, the cheaper they'll be, although keep an eye on stock to be careful not to miss out on the style or size that you want.

584 THINK BEFORE YOU SIGN

Before you sign up to membership cards, reward and discount programmes, do the sums – will joining actually save you money over the course of the year? You'll need to calculate how and when you'll actually be saving money and if it's worth it.

585 SOLE SINGER

Buying insoles for your shoes is a great way to extend their life and keep them comfortable. If you don't want to pay out for proper ones (even though it's a good investment) you can make your own out of several layers of newspaper.

586 BABY WALKS ALONE

Don't fall into the trap of buying expensive shoes for babies. Until children have learned to walk they don't need shoes. Bare feet are best for babies who are learning to walk because they will be able to feel the surface beneath them (they might need shoes for walking outside though).

587 BE VERSATILE

When children are young, there's no reason for them to have lots of pairs of shoes. Because children's feet are so delicate, it's better to spend money on a few good pairs of shoes that have been properly fitted, rather than lots of cheap ones that could hurt their feet.

588 BUY USED

If your children need dressy shoes for a special occasion, it's not worth spending a lot of money on them if they are only going to be worn once or twice. As they won't be worn often enough to affect a child's feet, it's OK to buy cheap or used shoes in this circumstance.

599 HIT THE RUBBER

Buying inexpensive stick-on rubber soles for your favourite shoes is a great way to preserve their life as shoes often begin to show the first signs of damage on the sole. Stick them on new soles to stop slips and to avoid damage. Check them regularly for worn areas.

600 BUSY BEE

You don't need to spend money on expensive shoe polishes – simply use the same beeswax-turpentine polish you use for your furniture (and the same goes for leather bags and gloves). Patent leather can be cleaned with petroleum jelly or even the inside of a banana skin.

601 POLISH THEM UP

Always polish your shoes regularly, even if you don't think they look like they need it. Polishing shoes is a great way to feed the leather and keep them supple and in good shape. That way, they'll last longer and won't start to look 'tired' until they really are!

602 READ THE REVIEWS

If you're thinking of buying shoes online it's worth reading reviews from other buyers before you commit to the purchase, especially as delivery costs can be high. Do your research and find out the best place to buy the shoes you want.

603 STEAM IT OUT

Steam is your friend when it comes to suede. Hold suede boots or gloves over the steam from a kettle (keeping your hands clear) and then simply brush them over to give them a freshen up. The same goes for bags and even clothes.

bath & beauty products

604 DRY YOUR BLADES

Razor blades will last longer if you dry them than leaving them to dry on their own.

605 GET A DISCOUNT

Discount stores are great places to buy soaps and body creams. They often have big names at low prices, so don't just buy clothes when you're out bargain hunting, take a minute to look at toiletries too.

606 SAVE YOUR BOTTLES

If you get samples or freebies from hotels or beauty counters, make sure you don't throw away the sample bottles. Clean them and fill them with your usual toiletries before you go on holiday (vacation), saving you money on buying miniature versions.

607 CUT OUT THE EXTRAS

Do you really need two different expensive creams for your eyes? You could save money by using an expensive cream every other day? Experiment with your routine and see if you notice changes after three or four weeks.

608 USE EVERY BIT

Instead of throwing away the toothpaste tube when you can't squeeze any more out, open it up with scissors to use every last bit.

609 BE TESTY

Ask for some small product testers before you buy. Most companies keep a stash under the counter to hand out to likely customers. Using the product in a variety of settings (home, work, outside, in the evening) will give you a chance to see if it's really right for you.

610 DON'T BE SPECIAL

Two for one – or even three for two – deals seem like a good idea at the time. But the only thing worse than being stuck with a bottle of moisturizer you can't use because it's too dry or greasy is being stuck with two of them! Only go for offers on products you know you'll use.

611 KEEP ON TRYING

Most women give up on new beauty purchases if they don't feel are getting results after about five uses, but experts say that this is not enough time to notice a visible effect. Your skin cells regenerate every four weeks, so it will take this long to see if a new product is working.

612 BE INVENTIVE

Just because your new moisturizer is too heavy for your face doesn't mean it won't work wonders on your dry elbows. Maybe that overly harsh facial scrub could leave your tired feet feeling lovely and soft? If a product doesn't work for the purpose that you bought it for, try using it in a different way.

613 THINK LATERALLY

Get creative and think of other ways to use unwanted products that don't work for you. For instance, shampoos and conditioners are great for handwashing wool or cashmere sweaters and will save you money on expensive specialist products.

614 ASK FOR A REFUND

If you have bought a beauty product because of promises made in advertisements or marketing and the product doesn't fulfil them, you're well within your rights to contact the supplier to see if they will offer you a refund. They may also refund for products that cause allergic reactions.

615 REDUCE YOUR AMOUNTS

Make sure you're not using too much product. The most common culprits for overuse are shower gel or cream, bath salts and shampoo. Try reducing the amount of product you use by half and see if you can tell the difference.

616 GET MULTIPLE

Buying two-in-one products is a great way to save money as you're only buying one bottle instead of two. This means you'll be using half the amount of product to get the same results. Common combinations include: sunscreen and body lotion; shampoo and conditioner; and cleanser and toner.

617 MULTITASKING

Astringent removes oil, dirt and make-up, unclogs pores and treats skin blemishes. But did you know that it can also be used as a remedy for burns, bites and stings? Also, if applied to nails prior to polishing, it helps to keep them clean and makes nail varnish last longer.

618 A LOTION FOR MANY USES

A cheap generic product, such as an unbranded baby lotion, is a great fallback item as it can be used as an everyday moisturizer and skin lotion as well as a cleanser, massage oil, shaving balm and even to control frizzy hair.

619 CHECK YOUR INGREDIENTS

Before you buy that expensive item, such as an eye cream or serum, check the generic names against the brand you are going to buy. If the ingredients list is the same, or nearly the same, you could save 50 per cent or more of the cost by buying generic or own-brand products instead.

620 A GOOD ALL-ROUNDER

One of the best buys for those trying beauty on a budget is a tub of petroleum jelly. Not only can it be used for beauty emergencies, like chapped lips, dried-out cuticles and split ends, it's also good for mixing make-up, protecting skin when you're applying beauty products and even for babies.

621 HAVE A BALL

If you use cotton wool balls, don't spend lots of money buying them already made. Simply buy an inexpensive roll of cotton wool and make your own balls. You can put them in an attractive jar or just keep the bag from the last lot you bought and reuse it.

622 FLOAT IN SALT

Epsom salts are a great choice for a relaxing, pampering bath, especially if your muscles are tired and they aren't pricey at all, so you're ticking all the boxes. Invest in the largest pot or packet you can to benefit from bulk buying.

623 PERFUMED AROMA

Instead of buying lots of products in the same scent as your perfume, use the perfume to make your own bath oil and body lotion. Adding a drop or two of your perfume (not eau de toilette) to unperfumed oil and lotion will help you feel expensive at a fraction of the price. Alternatively, mix a few drops of an essential oil into an inexpensive, unperfumed bath crème to make your own.

cosmetics

624 DON'T BE A WASTER

The total amount of money wasted on unfinished beauty products every year is staggering. If you've ever abandoned a foundation for being the wrong shade or discarded an eyeshadow because it looked better in its box than on you, you're contributing to this. Make it a rule to try before you buy, that way you won't buy products you're going to waste.

625 CHOOSE BROWN

Instead of buying an expensive brown eyeshadow, spend your money on a brown blusher instead and you'll get nearly twice the product for your money. You can use it as a blusher or shade/contour maker as well as an eyeshadow, which doubles your saving.

626 SAVE YOUR VARNISH (POLISH)

If your nail varnish (polish) has dried out, don't throw it away. Add a drop of nail varnish remover and shake the bottle well.

627 RECYCLE YOUR TOOTHBRUSH

Don't spend money on a special brush or comb for your eyebrows, simply spray a little hairspray or a dab of hairstyling gel on an old toothbrush and use that to shape them instead.

628 BUY RIGHT

When you're buying make-up think about how much you are going to use it. Most make-up doesn't last more than a year, so don't buy large amounts or you'll only end up throwing away.

629 BLUSH UP

Instead of spending lots of money on cream blushers, why not use your lipstick instead? Then, if you have several lipstick colours, you won't have to buy a blusher to match each one and you will always be colour coordinated. It can work the other way around, if your lipstick runs out.

630 LOVELY LASHES

Turn ordinary (cheaper) mascara into the lash-lengthening variety by dusting your lashes with loose translucent powder before you apply the mascara. This will help the mascara stick to the whole lash and is a great way to get the effect of an expensive product at a fraction of the price.

631 DON'T DISCARD

Instead of throwing your mascaras away when they become dry and clogged, save them and use the brush to tidy and colour eyebrows. Use an eyeshadow to fill in the brow line and simply brush through with your old mascara wand to avoid having to buy eyebrow colour or shapers.

632 PERFECT POWDER

To make your own loose powder simply mash up a cheap compact powder (choose one in a colour that is slightly darker than your skin tone) and put it in a sterilized jam jar or plastic pot with sealable lid. Mix in about twice as much baby powder and you'll have perfect face powder.

633 LONG-LASTING LIPPY

Don't throw away the end of your lipstick. Scrape it out of the container and heat it for a few seconds in the microwave; it will be useable again. Alternatively, combine it with petroleum jelly to make a tinted lip gloss. You can even mix a few of your favourite shades this way to create a new version.

634 AVOID FROSTING

Instead of buying frosted or glittery evening make-up, invest in a single frosted or shimmery powder and use it to augment your usual matt make-up. This way you can use it on our eyes, lips, cheeks or as a highlighter and you'll only be investing in one product.

635 GOOD FOUNDATION

Foundation is a really important part of your make-up routine so it's often a false economy to buy cheap products that don't work very well. It's better to spend a little more on a good foundation and wear it less. You'll find you need less of it anyway, because it will stay on your skin.

beauty treatments

636 SAMPLE IT

A great way to try out luxury make-up and perfume is to ask for samples. These are particularly good if you're going on a weekend trip or having girls' night in, as they will make you feel pampered for free. The best way to get samples is to ask the staff at the beauty counter questions – say you've got sensitive skin or want to try out an eye colour on a friend and they are more likely to offer you samples.

637 ADJUST YOUR POWDER

If your powder blusher is the wrong shade, don't throw it away. If it's too dark, simply mix in a little baby powder to lighten it or add a little brown blusher, eyeshadow or bronzer to make it darker.

638 SAND IT SHARP

Instead of throwing away tweezers when they become blunt, sharpen them yourself with sandpaper. Simply rub the sandpaper along the edges of the tweezers until you have a smooth, sharp surface, then wipe off the tweezers with a damp cloth or sponge.

639 BUST CELLULITE

For a cellulite-busting body scrub, keep your coffee grinds and mix in a handful with your usual shower gel. Because coffee contains caffeine, it is thought to help bust away cellulite and the oils it contains will also help keep your skin soft.

640 EPILATOR INVESTMENT

Instead of buying wax strips or visiting a salon, investing in an epilator is a great way to get hair removal on the cheap. Because you only pay out once for the machine (and it's roughly the same cost as one salon visit) your wallet will be laughing.

641 BE A BROW BEATER

When it comes to your eyebrows, inexperience can bring about bad results. The next time you get your brows professionally done keep them in shape by tweezing them regularly. With enough practice you'll soon learn how to do it yourself.

642 WAX AWAY

If you visit the beauty salon regularly for leg and/or bikini waxing, you could always try doing it yourself. Home-waxing kits are getting more and more effective, so it's worth trying. Or why not do your bikini yourself and go to the salon to have your legs done, then you might have to go less frequently.

643 TREAT AT HOME

Special beauty treatments at your local salon or day spa can be quite addictive, but extremely hazardous to your wallet. The main way to make the most of your beauty routine, while sparing your bank account, is to learn to do it yourself. If you can't, why not get a group of friends to help pamper each other?

644 NAIL IT

Visiting salons for manicures and pedicures is an expensive business, but do you really need to go so frequently? Watch what they do and get yourself a home manicure and pedicure kit. Make it more fun by doing it with friends. Initially, aim to cut your visits by half and see how you go from there.

haircare

645 FACE UP TO IT

Achieve a rich highlighted effect by going for colour highlights (or lowlights) around your face. It's cheaper than a whole or half head and it will make a real difference as the hair next to your face is what people notice most.

646 CUT THE COLOUR

High-maintenance colours – like light blonde or red – need frequent touch-ups that can be expensive. If you want to get great hair on a budget, it's best to stay as close to your natural colour as possible and choose scattered highlights so the roots won't show.

647 DITCH THE PROCESS

The more processes you have done to your hair, the more it will cost. If you want to go for colour, ask your colourist to change tonality with a single process or a gloss rather than changing the level of colour. Changing only the tone is far less expensive.

648 GET A STUDENT CUT

Student hairdressers will often give you a free haircut if you let them practise their 'up-dos' and other styling on you. Some offer knock-down prices for junior stylists-in-training too, and it could save you on regular cuts. Ask at your local beauty school.

649 WASH LESS OFTEN

If you shampoo your hair every day, you will remove all the natural oils from your scalp, which can dry it out and make it itch, which can make you shampoo even more often. Try to shampoo every two or three days so your scalp has a chance to heal and you use less shampoo.

650 USE LESS SHAMPOO

A good way to help reduce product build-up is to add a teaspoon of bicarbonate of soda (baking soda) to your shampoo. You will then use less shampoo as your hair will feel cleaner and healthier.

651 AT-HOME COLOUR

The cheapest way to colour your hair is to do it yourself at home, but don't feel you have to stick to what's on the box. You can mix two formulas (though its best to stick to the same brand) to create your own unique colour – go for darker tones on the underlayers or back and lighter at the top or front of your hair.

652 GET 'FLASH'

Extend the life of your colour (and reduce expensive trips to the hair salon) by asking for a 'flash' between highlighting appointments – this will help preserve the colour in your hair so you have to visit for a complete overhaul less often.

653 SPLURGE ON SHAMPOO

A good-quality shampoo does not contain detergent ingredients that strip hair, so if you are budgeting it's more important you buy a good shampoo than conditioner. Conditioners are pretty much universal in their hair-smoothing offerings, so don't worry about trying cheaper version of this.

654 TRY A CHEAPIE

A little-known industry secret is that some of the more expensive lines usually have cheaper versions. Brands like L'Oreal, TRESemmé and Aveda all have reasonably priced, but effective, alternative products.

655 BE A MODEL

Most good salons host model nights where master stylists oversee up-and-coming stylists as they practise their skills. Usually, there are separate cutting and colouring events, so make sure your stylist knows you are interested or call other good salons and ask to be put on the 'modelling list'.

656 BOB IT

A style with very little layering or that is just one length, such as a bob, is stylish and will keep its shape as it grows, making frequent trims unnecessary. Start with a chin-length bob as it will still look good when it has grown to your shoulders. This will mean around six months between haircuts, just think of the saving!

657 BLOW IT DRY

Invest in a good blow-dryer because if you get a quality dryer it will mean less investment in extra hairstyling tools like straightening irons and curling tongs. With a good hairdryer, pretty much all styles should be achievable.

658 CHIN DOWN

If you have opted for a money-saving bob your stylist should ask you at some point to tip your head down, chin to chest. They will then trim off any stray hairs that appear at the nape area. If they don't ask you to do this, you should ask them, as it improves the wearability of your bob and lengthens the time it will keep its shape.

659 WET CUT

Leaving the salon with wet or roughly dried hair is almost always cheaper than letting the stylist dry and style it for you. The downside is you don't get to see the finished look, but for long-hair trims and bobs this can be a great choice.

660 CHOOSE QUALITY

Go to a good salon, use an experienced stylist and have a simple cut. Explain to the stylist that you need something low maintenance because of financial restrictions. Ask for a cut that will be easy to maintain and require infrequent salon visits and they will go through your options.

luxuries for less

661 DVDS TO YOUR DOOR

Mail-order DVD rental is a great home entertainment option. You sign up with a service (the cost depends on how many DVDs you wish to view per month), then list the DVDs you want to rent. Your choices are then mailed to you. Each time you finish one, you send it back in the prepaid envelope and the service sends you another from your list. No late fees, no waiting in line and it's usually cheaper than your local film store.

662 GET A MAKEOVER

Most make-up companies or concession counters in department stores offer makeovers, but many of them charge, so check the terms. The money you spend is, however, usually redeemable against purchases. Wait until your make-up runs out and you need to spend money, then arrange a makeover. As you would have spent the money anyway it's practically free!

663 GET IT HOME DELIVERED

Pretty much everything can be found online for home delivery. Compare prices, check delivery charges and think about the most sensible things to order online.

664 INDULGE IN A MASSAGE

You don't need to go for a full day at a spa to benefit from a pampering massage. Find a massage therapist who will come to your home, it will be much cheaper than going to a salon. You could even call the local beauty school to offer your services to massage students who need to practise to perfect their technique.

665 ITS A WRAP

A great way to get a luxury look for pennies when you are wrapping presents is to buy tissue paper (in bulk) and rolls of clear cellophane (cheap from your local florist or flower stall). Loosely wrap the item in tissue paper first, then sprinkle petals, leaves or other found items over it before covering the whole thing with clear cellophane and tying it with a ribbon.

666 VISIT A NAIL BAR

Manicures and pedicures are far cheaper at nail bars than they are at salons, and they take less time too, although the experience isn't often relaxing. Limit your salon visits to once or twice a year and visit nail bars the rest of the time to keep your nails looking good.

667 PAMPERED PETS

If you usually get your dog groomed by a professional groomer, try doing it yourself. You can get training through a home study programme or class, which will save you a lot of cash. As for those pricey gourmet doggie biscuits, the diamanté collars and the acupuncture for your sulky cat, well you know where you can make a cutback!

668 USE A TAX PROFESSIONAL

There are some areas where saving the pennies isn't as important as doing a thorough job. One of them is your tax return so make sure you use a professional or seek professional advice. Using someone in the know will always help you in the long run.

669 GO SMALL

You might have to cut down on luxuries to balance the books, but you don't have to forego them completely. Think creatively about how to include a little luxury in your life. A cashmere jumper, for instance, might be out of the question, but gloves and a hat cost far less.

670 THINK PERSONAL

If you think personal shoppers are only for the rich and famous, think again. Many larger branches of cheaper chain stores have a style advisory service. Usually all you need to do is make an appointment online or by phone. This is a great way to feel pampered while you shop, and usually there is no fee.

671 BAG A PACKAGE

Spa resorts and day spas often run special offers during the week so if you can get away (preferably with a friend or partner to share a room if you're staying overnight) on a Tuesday or Wednesday the price is likely to be much lower. Ask the resorts about how to get the cheapest deal.

672 EAT OUT FOR LESS

In the summer months, many newspapers and magazines run special voucher offers where you can collect a certain number of vouchers to get a two-for-one meal, or some other such offer. Usually the offers are for midweek dining so it's worth planning ahead.

673 SCENT-SATIONAL FRAGRANCE

If designer labels for clothes and handbags are out of your reach, consider opting for a designer fragrance instead, it will give you a little boost of luxury without the financial outlay of a high-priced couture item. Nearly all well-known names offer a fragrance range.

674 TAKE TEA

A great way to get that pampered restaurant feeling at a fraction of the cost is to go out for afternoon tea, the meal often comes with champagne as well as tea and coffee and is substantial enough for you to skip lunch beforehand. Plus, it's often a third or even half the price of a nice lunch or dinner.

675 IN THE CLUB

Do an online search (or ask your fashionista friends) for clubs that run private sales of designer clothes, usually at the end of a season. Often, you can get clothes at up to 80 per cent off the asking price, and because not many people know about them you can often grab great bargains.

676 FREE FACIAL

A relaxing facial is the ultimate in decadence, but you don't have to pay top price. Ask around at your local beauty school as they usually offer huge discounts on salon prices. And don't worry about being a guinea pig, you are likely to be treated by a final-year student close to graduation.

677 BID UP

As long as you don't suffer from auction fever, TV and online auctions are a great way to buy items like jewellery and home furnishings, as well as designer clothes. Make sure you have a list of what you want before you shop and keep a partner or friend with you so you don't get carried away.

678 ASK FOR GIFTS

If you're being budget conscious, you're likely to have crossed those pampering luxury toiletries off your shopping list, but you can add them to your gift list so you can still have them a few times a year and really enjoy the treat.

679 TRAVEL FIRST CLASS

Depending on the rail service in your country, a great way to get yourself a first-class seat, while paying for standard class, can be to take a meal on the train. The restaurant car is even more comfortable than first class and if you buy a meal you can stretch out in style – better than a sandwich in your standard seat!

dinner parties

680 MAKE A SUBSTITUTE

If you want your dinner party to be fabulous, without costing the earth, make substitutes. You could use Arenkha (a combination of smoked herring with squid ink, lemon juice and spices) instead of caviar, smoked trout for smoked salmon, truffle oil instead of truffles, and rib of beef instead of fillet.

681 SHARE THE LOAD

A great way to have dinner parties on the cheap is to ask your friends to each bring a dish. It's a good way to spread cost and you'll get a range of different foods, which is always entertaining.

682 SERVE A SIDE ORDER

Grains, such as couscous, barley and rice, can make delicious (and very cheap) side dishes. Don't just boil them and serve – be more imaginative and blend them with a spicy dressing, soak in stock (broth) or cook them slowly with some peas to make a rich pilaf.

683 FLAVOURS FROM THE EAST

While a French-inspired dinner might feel odd without fish or meat, cuisines with vegetarian or semi-vegetarian traditions like Indian, Thai and Japanese offer loads of budget-friendly non-meat recipes. Concentrate on one central bean- or noodle-based dish, with multiple, simple, colourful vegetarian side dishes.

684 SPANISH FIZZ INSTEAD OF FRENCH

Instead of offering champagne at your next party, make up a cocktail using cava. Kir is a great addition or you could add a mixture of fruit juices. Try less common flavours like ruby orange and pomegranate for a different taste.

685 BBQ BASHES

An outdoor barbecue party is an easy, low-cost form of entertaining. Burgers, sausages or hot dogs, as well as skewers of chicken and/or vegetables are all inexpensive to buy and quick to cook. As the occasion is informal and outdoors, you don't need to worry about decorations or fancy tableware.

686 SERVE IT UP

Instead of serving individual portions, eat family-style with guests serving themselves from large platters. It's more efficient and it makes big curries and stews look as if they're designed for fun dining, not to save money.

687 BIG UP DESSERT

Serving a good dessert is key to a successful dinner party, but it doesn't have to be expensive. Chocolate mousse is a great choice because, although it uses eggs and good-quality chocolate that are both a bit pricey, it's so rich you don't need much of it. Or go for fruit crumbles or pies with ice cream and cream.

688 ONE FABULOUS COCKTAIL

Instead of buying lots of different bottles of wine, beer and spirits, stick to one choice or, even more budget conscious, a simple cocktail. That way, you can buy the ingredients in bulk rather than bits here and there.

689 BRING A BOTTLE

Make up a couple of cheap cocktail bases, such as mint syrup and fruit juice punch, then ask your guests to bring a mixer of their own choice for your pre-dinner cocktails. Or buy the booze yourself and ask them to bring along the mixers they like.

690 BUY CHEAP CUTS

A dinner party is a great opportunity to cook a cheaper cut of meat. The meat might need a bit of extra attention and longer cooking, but cheaper cuts are perfect for casseroles and stews, which can be cooked the day before and left to develop a more mature flavour. This means a cheaper meal and less work for you on the night.

691 PLANT A DECORATION

Instead of spending money on flowers to create a centrepiece for the table, use one of your houseplants instead or make your own artificial flowers from tissue paper. Another cheap alternative is a glass bowl filled with pine cones, dried leaves or twigs.

692 GIN UP ON FLAVOUR

A great way to give your guests interesting after-dinner liqueurs is to flavour gin by adding fruit (and sugar to taste) to the bottle. Sour fruits work well, such as sloes and cranberries – buy them in season when they are at their cheapest. The bottle can be left for months to allow the flavour to develop.

693 AFTER-DINNER LIQUEUR

Make your own coffee liqueur from equal measures of milk and cream with a dash of coffee syrup and whisky to taste. This is a much cheaper alternative to buying expensive bottles of liqueur you won't use and because you only make as much as you need, there's no waste.

694 SUP A SOUP

Soup is a great inexpensive choice for the first course of a dinner party, but you don't have to stick to serving it in bowls. Use teacups for a cute look or shot glasses for a more modern approach, particularly if the soup is a vivid colour. If you are using bowls, add some cream and chopped herbs to jazz it up.

695 SPOON IT UP

Instead of spending lots of money on expensive finger foods, make your budget canapés look a million dollars by serving them arranged on slate or wooden boards. You could even put each one on the tip of a teaspoon so guests can grab and go.

696 SOCIABLE FOOD

Instead of having a sit-down meal, why not serve an Indian buffet or tapas? These are great cheap foods because you can mix a few good ingredients in with lots of 'bulkers', such as chickpeas and potatoes, to give the appearance of luxury without the budget-busting expense.

687 FOOD FOR ALL SEASONS

The best way to cook a dinner party on a budget is – surprise, surprise – to use ingredients that are in season. Winter is a great time for hearty casseroles, summer for salads and what better in autumn than a fruit crumble. That way, your ingredients will cost less.

dining & drinking

688 GET A TOP TABLE

Getting a special deal at a 'destination' restaurant can be tricky as they are often booked up months ahead of time. However they may have a table at an unusual time slot, such as 11am, which may be perfect for a special occasion or working brunch. Many of the exclusive restaurants have cheaper lunch menus so always call and ask. Also look at websites such as www. toptable.co.uk, which lists special offers for fine dining internationally.

689 EAT BREAKFAST OUT

If you can't give up your eating-out habit, opt for breakfast instead of lunch or dinner. Breakfast is far cheaper than other meals and will give you fuel to last the day. Many hotels offer special breakfast deals as will already be serving the people who are staying there.

700 HAVE A HAPPY HOUR

Get to know the bars and restaurants that offer happy hour; not only will the drinks be cheaper, usually half price, but the establishment often offers free nibbles and cut-price food during the same time period too.

701 PARTY OF TWO

If you're going out for a meal, make it a rule to stick to two courses. If necessary, have a snack on your way home from work or before you leave the house so that you don't feel too hungry, then you'll be happy just to choose two courses at the restaurant.

702 CHECK ONLINE

The Internet is a great resource for dinner deals. Lots of sites are dedicated to offering vouchers that give you money off or deals on your meal. Make sure you print out the voucher and take it along with you to ensure the restaurant gives you what you're entitled to and check at the beginning of your meal exactly what the terms are.

703 MAKE FRIENDS WITH THE MAÎTRE D'

If you go to a particular restaurant regularly, make sure the maître d' gets to know you. Their job is to allocate tables and usually there are a certain number set aside for last-minute regulars or celebrities. The maître d' is your way to a good table and a reservation. If you build up their trust they will let you know if there are any special deals and which entrées are value for money.

704 EAT IN AND OUT

Eating out usually costs two to three times as much as preparing meals at home. Set yourself a spending limit that fits with your budget for the month and try to spread your eating out across the month so you don't tire of being at home.

705 CUT THE BOOZE

Alcohol has a huge markup, and it's often the drink that constitutes the major percentage of your meal costs. If you really want a drink, sharing a bottle of house wine is the best way to go, or drink bottled beer instead.

706 FILL UP ON FREEBIES

Choose restaurants that offer free food or nibbles before your meal arrives. Bread, olives and other hors d'oeuvres are good choices as they will fill you up and stop you ordering an appetizer, which means you save money on your meal.

707 CLICK BEFORE YOU LEAVE

Before you go out to eat, always remember to check the website of the restaurant you're going to. This is quite separate from online discount vouchers, but often restaurants will run their own discount deals exclusively to online customers, so it's worth looking. Sign up to your favourite chains for a newsletter or email alert on special deals.

708 KEEP IT SIMPLE

Often the simplest things on the menu are the cheapest, so those are the ones to go for if you are on a really strict budget. But if you find you're ordering food you don't really like because it's all you can afford, maybe you'd be better staying at home?

708 A DOGGY BAG

Instead of leaving your leftover food, take it with you so you can use it for another meal. If you're embarrassed to ask for a doggy bag, take Tupperware with you. You wouldn't dream of leaving half the food you've paid for in a store, so why do it in a restaurant?

710 GO MIDWEEK

Many restaurants offer specials on weekday evenings to help bring people in during their slower times. Since most people typically only eat out at the weekend they don't take advantage of this, so get to know which restaurants in your area do specials, but avoid the chef's night off, which is usually Monday.

711 HAVE A HAPPY BIRTHDAY

Eating out on your birthday is a great money-saving idea, as long as you tell the restaurant before you arrive. Many offer deals such as a free dessert, drink or even meal, so make sure you research it and give them notice ahead of time.

712 KEEP CARDS TO HAND

Many restaurants and coffee shops operate loyalty or gift card systems, but how many times have you left your cards at home? Keep all your loyalty cards in a special section of your wallet that you can see easily so they are always visible and on hand to help you save.

713 SPLIT THE COSTS

A good way to cut down on what you spend in a restaurant is to go easy on the alcohol, but this can be a problem if you're splitting the cost with friends who aren't similarly frugal. At the beginning of the meal ask for two separate bills (checks), one for food and one for alcohol, then those who don't drink aren't stung with the cost.

714 CHECK OUT A BYOB RESTAURANT

Why not eat out at a place where you can take your own alcohol? Often, the food is just as good as a typical restaurant, but because you take your own booze there's no astronomical drinks cost. Check beforehand for corkage charges, though.

715 EAT BEFORE YOU GO

If you're going out drinking in the evening, make sure you have a good meal before you set off, not only because it's sensible, but also because you're less likely to make expensive food decisions later.

717 TAKE YOUR OWN

Many cinemas actually make the majority of their profit from food. Providing it doesn't break the rules, take your own drinks, popcorn and sweets (candy) from home.

theatre, concerts & cinema

716 ADMIRE THE VIEW

If you want to attend music concerts, sporting events and so on, but can't afford tickets, why not volunteer? Ushers and helpers often get to see the entertainment or event for free in return for a small wage and a couple of hours of work. Investigate your local options.

718 GO OUT EARLY

If you want to visit the cinema, but can't afford a full-price movie ticket try the matinee showings in the afternoon that can be a lot cheaper. Also look for free film viewings at church halls and other meeting places.

719 BOOK DIRECT

Whenever you're booking a ticket it's usually cheaper to reserve directly with the venue, where they will often offer cut-price tickets even if you book in advance. You should always try this approach, even if you're directed to an agency, because cutting out the middlemen is almost always cheaper.

720 GO IN PERSON

If you are booking tickets for somewhere nearby, go to the box office in person. Staff will often spend longer looking for deals for you if you're standing in front of them and you can often negotiate a lower booking fee, plus you'll save on delivery costs, so everyone's a winner.

721 STRIKE A DEAL

Some theatres offer deals that are linked to transportation. If you have taken the bus, for instance, or have a valid train ticket for that day you can sometimes get a special offer, like two for one or a discount off the price. These are usually midweek deals, but they can add up to significant savings.

722 VERIFY THE WEBSITE

Before you book theatre tickets online through the theatre's website, take a few minutes to make sure it is actually the theatre's official website. In recent years, unscrupulous companies have started making close copies of the theatres' own websites to fool people into paying higher prices that they need to.

723 BOOST A BOOTH

In many big cities there are official half-price ticket booths to whom the theatres sell off their unwanted tickets for that day. It's always worth checking these booths if you're buying the tickets on the day and they're a great choice if you can be flexible.

724 DON'T SAY 'OFFER'

If you have a theatre offer from a newspaper or magazine that requires you to quote a code, make sure you don't mention the deal straightaway when you call them. To begin with, tell them which seats you'd like to book and on what day. See which seats they offer you and only then mention your special offer code or deal. This way they won't try and off-load the cheaper and not so good seats on you just because they're 'deal' tickets.

725 SAME-DAY TICKET

Often, theatres will keep back some seats and offer them for sale on the morning of the performance. These are usually at a discount, so if you don't mind getting up early and queuing for the box office to open, it can be a great cheap way to buy theatre tickets. When you are making your plans though, bear in mind that you might not be lucky if lots of other people have the same idea and there aren't enough tickets to go round, so always have alternative plans in place.

726 STANDBY FOR CONCESSIONS

Most theatres and cinemas offer concessions for older people, students and people with disabilities, but the savings can be even bigger if you are prepared to wait until the last few hours before the performance. Often, they will give concession standby seats for as much as 70 per cent off, so it's really worth giving them a call if you can get there within a few hours.

buying gifts

727 CHECK YOUR GIFT STASH

Keep a list of who you need to buy presents for each month and make sure you go through your store of presents from time to time to make sure perishable things, such as chocolates, don't go out of date. There's no point buying up offers for presents if you don't use them in time and end up throwing them away.

728 STOCK UP IN JANUARY

January is a great month for stocking up on gifts as the stores and supermarkets often have all their Christmas merchandise on sale. Avoid anything overtly Christmassy (unless you can keep it for a year!). Go for generic presents that you can use for people's birthdays throughout the coming year.

729 ITS A WRAP

Create your own unique cheap wrapping paper using inexpensive rolls of brown paper and stamping patterns on them. Make your own stamps from old sponges or potatoes and dot the pattern all over the paper for a unique and budget gift wrap. Finish with a big ribbon.

730 BUY SECOND-HAND

Kids don't care if the things that you buy them are second-hand. While adults might not appreciate a previously used gift, take advantage of the fact that your kids don't care by buying second-hand toys when they're young, particularly for Christmas stockings or party prizes.

731 PRINT YOUR OWN CARDS

Making your own greetings cards is a great way to save money. Use photos for a collage or design your own look on the computer and print it out. Buy card and coloured envelopes in bulk and you'll make even more of a saving. Try children's craft stores for cheap glue and other materials.

732 CHEAPER POSTAGE

Before you buy those first class stamps, does the card really need to get there a day sooner? Buying second class will suffice for most postage items (you'll just have to think ahead a little if it's a birthday or Christmas gift). Alternatively, send a

postcard rather than greetings cards and letters as they are less expensive to post.

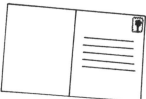

733 KEEP KIDS' STUFF IN RESERVE

If you've got kids you'll be expected to find gifts at the drop of a hat, every time someone in their class has a birthday, in fact! If you can, do some canny bulk buying of materials, such as beads and wire that you can separate and make into individual bead-making kits. The same goes for craft items like pens, stickers and coloured papers.

734 RAID THE BINS

Raid bargain bins at your local charity (thrift) store to unearth interesting bits of material, costume jewellery and other items you could use for cards. Look for clothes with beading, sequins and interesting buttons that you could use for decoration.

735 PICTURE PERFECT GIFT

A great choice of gift for older relatives is one of the simplest ideas on the planet – a photo of a loved one (grandchildren and great grandchildren are always favourites). You can personalize it by customizing a cheap photo frame yourself.

736 BE A NEWSHOUND

Instead of buying expensive gift-wrapping paper, use newspaper and buy a large roll of cheap ribbon from a local store to tie a bow on top. It's an attractive and different way to wrap your gifts.

737 RECYCLE CARDS

If someone sends you a card you like, don't throw it away. Keep it to copy or even cut the front off and reuse it to create a new card. Just remember not to send your reused version back to the person who sent you the original card!

738 STASH YOUR GIFTS

Start a gift drawer. Stock it with three-for-two offers and sale items. You can store up so you don't get caught out having to buy expensive items later.

739 PRESENTS FOR FREE

There are loads of Internet sites that you can register with to receive freebies. A good tip is to keep anything you manage to get in this way to use as presents. That way, you'll stock up on gifts without spending a penny. Keep extra samples or goody bags you get when you buy cosmetics or other products, as they will come in handy for gifts.

740 RE-GIFT

If someone gives you a gift you don't like or won't use, don't be afraid to recycle it. Giving it to someone else is a great way to save money and because everyone's taste is different, they might love something you wouldn't have used.

741 KEEP YOUR DRAWER SHUT

Once you have set up your gift drawer, remember its purpose: it's designed to save you money on gifts you would have had to buy, not to be used for extras. Don't hand them out if you wouldn't have bought a gift anyway.

742 COLOURFUL TISSUES

Tissue paper is your best friend when it comes to making cheap gifts look expensive. Invest in a bulk buy of different colours and use it throughout the year to help you wrap up gifts, form bases for hampers and for use in crafts as well.

743 USE YOUR POINTS

Why not make it a rule that you will use all the points you amass from loyalty cards to buy gifts? Your gift drawer will be full before you know it.

homemade gifts & baskets

744 MAKE GIFT CARDS

Instead of buying gift cards, use old Christmas and birthday cards cut down with decorative scissors or cut into patterns. Simply write on the back and attach it with a ribbon or string.

745 MAKE A CARD BOX

In a box or drawer, keep all the things you could use to make your own greetings cards – tissue, glitter, scraps of wrapping paper and ribbon (salvaged from presents), old photos, pictures from magazines and newspapers and anything else you could use to make creative cards.

746 PRESS SOME FLOWERS

Pressed flowers are a great way to decorate cards and presents. Pick them in season and press them under a pile of books between sheets of tissue or kitchen paper towels and in a few months you'll have perfect free decorations.

747 BAKE IT AT HOME

Homemade foods make great gifts, such as chocolates, jams, cakes and cookies, if they're packaged right. Give chocolates in little organza bags that you can pick up for pennies online, or use flat-pack bakery boxes and tissue paper for larger items.

748 WORKS OF ART

Kids' drawings can be used to make great presents. For example, scan pieces of artwork and use them to make a calendar or a notepad with different designs on each page. Computer-design programmes make this kind of gift accessible to everyone, not just the professionals.

749 GLASSY EYED

For a present with a difference, buy some glass paint and a couple of cheap glasses from a discount store or supermarket, then get creative. You could also use this idea for glass serving bowls and plates, even mirrors.

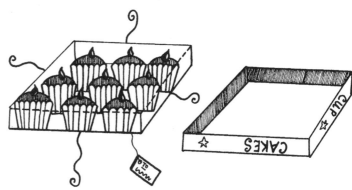

751 TAKE A CUTTING

Here's a gift idea that might take you a bit of time, but that will be gratefully received by any keen gardener. Take some cuttings from your favourite plants, grow them into small plants, then package them up in attractive pots and give them away as unique gifts. This is also an easy way for you to create more houseplants without buying new ones. Use a scissors or a razor blade, sterilized in alcohol, to take a cutting just below a leaf node. A single node with a couple of leaves is enough.

752 BE A SERVANT

Why not give someone the gift of being their servant for the day? Set any rules you want, but what better present to give a busy friend or family member than a whole (or half) day of your time to do their chores for them. It's also a great cashless choice for giving. Alternatively, give a 'promise' coupon – kids could promise to wash their parents' car, parents could cook a 'meal of choice', and partners could give a pampering massage or foot rub.

750 FOR CHOCOLATE LOVERS

Why not make up a chocolate-lovers hamper as an inexpensive, but thoughtful, gift? Put in sachets of hot chocolate, a few chocolate bars (buy them when they are on offer), some marshmallows and even a cheap mug and tie them all up in bulk-bought tissue or cellophane.

753 LUXURY BATH SALTS

Instead of buying expensive bath salts for people, make your own by layering Epsom salts, dried rose petals and essential oils in a glass jar or bottle. If you put it in a pretty box, it will be as luxurious as any store-bought gift.

754 SWEET TREATS

Hampers are a great way to give budget presents that are thoughtful and look expensive, while costing a minimum amount of money. Make up a grocery hamper for a general gift, with homemade jam, bread and cookies. Or think about a themed hamper, the more imaginative the better.

755 WHAT KIDS LIKE

When you're giving presents to kids, think about what they would like rather than being seduced by flashing lights on plastic toys and computer games. For instance, a nature-loving child might like a personalized basket containing a magnifying glass, an insect spotter book and a nesting box for the garden.

756 BE A VALENTINE

For a great gift for St Valentine's Day, make up a 'love' hamper. Give sexy gifts like underwear and cologne, or a romantic version with champagne and a framed photo. Include scented candles and massage oil and don't forget that' I owe you a massage' voucher!

757 BOX OF MEMORIES

If you're attending a special event, such as a wedding or christening, and can't afford a gift, why not make a 'memory box'? Include a newspaper from that day, the cork from the champagne and a few photographs of the day's important events to create a cheap, but thoughtful, present.

758 FOR FOODIES

A food hamper is the ideal gift for food aficionados, and the more exotic the ingredients the better. Depending on their tastes, consider chilli peppers (fresh, dried, pickled and in sauces and relishes), spices (different powders, spices, accompaniments), or for an Italian theme try dried porcini mushrooms, truffle oil and arborio rice.

759 JAMS AND PRESERVES

Free food is more bountiful than you think. Collect berries from the wild to make your own jams and preserves for a thoughtful and unique gift. Alternatively use them to make cakes or muffins and freeze any that are left over.

760 A GIFT OF RELAXATION

Why not make some luxurious, but inexpensive, bath oils to give to a friend or family member? Reuse old bottles or buy inexpensive ones from charity (thrift) stores or discount stores, fill them with a basic oil, such as light olive or almond oil, and add a few drops of essential oil. Try lavender for relaxation, citrus for boosting energy and rose for calming.

761 THINK OF YOUR MOTHER

Make a box or basket for your mother on Mother's Day containing her favourite foods, scented candles, and so on. Think about her hobbies: include seed packets or hand cream if she's a gardener; a new (handmade if you like) apron or tea towel if she's a cook; or simply a couple of magazines, a sachet of bath oil and a miniature bottle of cava!

762 JET-SETTER'S HAMPER

This is the perfect gift for a friend who's always on the move. Keep all those freebie shampoos, conditioners, foundations and moisturizers, even the lipsticks that come free with magazines and the sample bottles you are given in hotels (as long as they don't have the name of the hotel on the bottle), then organize them into a 'travel' beauty hamper. You could also buy small plastic bottles and pots and decant products into them.

763 RECIPE IN A JAR

Give a gift your recipient can use to make something they really love – this suggestion is especially good for kids. Layer measured amounts of marshmallows, crushed cookies, chocolate, cherries and dried fruits in a glass jar and stick a label on the outside with the extra ingredients they will need and the method to make their very own rocky road chocolate bar. Use the same idea for cakes, cookies, muffins and any other recipe you want to hand on as a gift.

music & films

764 WATCH A LAPTOP

You don't need an expensive television and DVD player to watch films. If your laptop has a DVD/CD player you can watch DVDs on your laptop instead. Most laptops have the same standard of graphics as high-definition TVs.

765 LISTEN ONLINE

Instead of investing lots of money in a stereo system, listen to your music through your computer. Most computer speakers are good enough quality, but if you're a real music lover investing in a good pair of speakers to plug into your computer is still cheaper than buying a whole stereo system.

766 DOWNLOAD YOUR MUSIC

If you're not already buying your music online and downloading it into a music management programme, start now. Albums are around 30 per cent cheaper to buy as downloads and you won't have the problem of where to store them.

767 SWAP CDS

Instead of spending money on new CDs, why not exchange your old CDs for credit at your local music store next time you want to invest in a new album? That way, you can continue to change your CD collection without actually parting with any money (particularly if you've downloaded them as well, that way you can still listen).

768 GROUP UP

Rent DVDs from a store as a group, then you can pass the disc around so that everyone can watch it within the agreed time. It's important you don't give it back late though, as the fine will negate the saving. Take turns to watch it first so nobody gets last place all the time.

769 DOWNLOAD FOR FREE

If you're a music lover and you're not afraid to experiment, there are a lot of places online that allow you to download copyright-free music. Mostly it will be the work of new and upcoming artists, but it's a great way to get an unusual library of music together and to impress your friends by being the first to discover new talent!

770 USE THE LIBRARY

Your local library isn't just for books and magazines, it's also a great place to rent movies and CDs, particularly the classics. You can watch films and listen to music for free, as long as you return the items on time so that you don't incur charges.

771 SHARE THE MUSIC

Swap your CDs with friends. Agree to swap around four or five CDs each month and work on a rotation system so that every month you get a new collection of music to listen to.

772 TRY BEFORE YOU BUY

Choose an online music subscription service that gives you the opportunity to demo the music you are interested in. This means that you only have to buy the tracks and albums that you are going to enjoy, so you won't waste your money buying music you are not interested in and won't listen to.

773 SELL USED DVDS, CDS AND GAMES

Your local DVD rental store might buy or part-exchange your used DVDs, especially if they are popular films. Music and gaming stores may also take your old CDs and computer games, if they are in good condition. Alternatively you can use eBay, or any other online auction site, or the advertisements in your local paper to sell unwanted games, films or music.

books, newspapers & magazines

774 BE A MAGAZINE SUBSCRIBER

The best way to save money if you are a magazine buyer is to take out a subscription. Make sure you take advantage of any special offers – a free first magazine, for example – and always haggle with them to try to get more money off.

775 SHARE IT OUT

The chances are you and your friends buy and read the same magazines or books. Why not agree that each of you will buy one magazine and them pass it around each other on rotation each month. Swap around every three months so you take turns to read different magazines first.

776 DON'T PAY EARLY

When it comes to magazine subscriptions, it's a buyers market – they want your subscription and that puts you in a good bargaining position. Don't be tempted to re-new early when it runs out, hang on until the last minute and you'll get better offers to stay.

777 GO ONLINE

There is loads of free information available online. If you wait a few weeks many magazines make their articles available on the Web after they're published in print. The great feature here is that you can search by keywords to find articles you're interested in and bookmark the page, which is tidier than a pile of cuttings.

778 DARE TO DISCOUNT

Certain companies offer newspaper subscriptions at a discounted rate, which are usually much lower (sometimes up to half as much) than the rates offered directly from the publisher. Always check discount prices before you sign up to a publisher's subscription though.

779 USE A LIBRARY

If you're trying to save money, the public library could be your best friend. Not only will it help you save money on books, they also usually have a range of newspapers and magazines. If they don't have the one you want, why not ask them if they can get it?

780 SUBSCRIPTION GIFT

Often, relatives and friends don't know what to buy you as gifts. Why not ask for a magazine subscription or money towards one? It's an easy gift for them to give and will last you all year long.

781 BE A NEWBIE

To qualify for new subscriber rates, even if you are already subscribed, cancel your subscription temporarily and then use your spouse or partner's name as the new customer. Alternatively, simply ask them to match the deal.

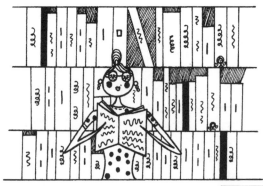

782 CONSIDER YOUR PURCHASE

Before you grab your favourite magazine from the rack at the supermarket or newsagent, have a quick look through it and see if it's really worth paying for. You might find that it actually won't hold your interest for long and it's not worth the outlay.

783 SELL THEM ON

Don't just throw your magazines away when you've finished with them, especially if you get a subscription that means you'll get them early. Sell them when you've read them, after about two weeks, for half the price. This works well with neighbours and friends, particularly if they don't mind reading it a few weeks after you. Make sure you keep them in good condition.

784 READ AND RECYCLE

If you take your magazines to a recycling depot, the next time you go check the piles that other people have left to see if there are any there that you'd like to read. For security, remember to remove your name and address if you get subscriptions in case other people pick your magazines up.

785 EBAY MAGAZINES

If you've never thought about buying magazines on eBay, here's your chance to try. eBay has a thriving magazine section and often the charges are half the cover price. Keep an eye on shipping costs though and try to find a seller who ships for free.

786 NEWSPAPER TO YOUR DOOR

It's not only magazines you can get on subscription, why not try subscribing to newspapers too? It's easy and could save you up to half the money you would spend if you were buying directly from a newsstand or kiosk.

787 TAKE A LONG VIEW

Almost all newspapers offer a discount to subscribers who commit to longer periods of time, usually the longer you commit, the cheaper it will be each year. It sounds intimidating to sign up for long periods of time, but think about what is really going to change. Unless you're going to move house, it's likely that you'll want to keep subscribing so go for it!

788 BURN IT UP

Instead of throwing old newspapers and magazines away, why not buy a machine to turn them into briquettes you can use on your fire as fuel. It's a great way to use up old paper and will save you money on fuel costs too.

computers & electronics

789 CANCEL TRIALS

If you aren't interested in continuing, cancel trials after they have expired. Trial offers are not just there to let customers try the product or service; the company relies on a certain number of lazy customers who sign up and forget about them. Longer trials (30 days or more) are especially useful for seeing just how much use you'll get out of something. If the answer is very little, make sure you cancel before you are charged.

780 DECLINE WARRANTIES

Your computer should be under manufacturer's warranty for the first year anyway, so spending lots of money on an extended warranty from the store or manufacturer is usually not worth the money. Companies make an astounding profit off these schemes, which probably means it's not that good for customers.

781 GET A FIREWALL

You're likely to head off future repair bills if you protect your computer investment with antivirus software and a firewall. Try getting the store to add them for free, as they often have deals with antivirus companies.

782 COMPUTER RECYCLING

You can't throw old computers away, they have to be recycled, which typically costs you money. Facilities that recycle usually charge for their disposal services, but it's worth asking the manufacturer if they offer a recycling programme. Wherever you go, it's important to get your hard drive degassed, which erases the contents.

783 GO ONLINE

When you're shopping for software, the most expensive way to buy it is in a store. Search the Internet for freeware and shareware sites that offer low-cost products, and look for special offers and deals on the software you want to buy.

784 BUY A QUALITY PRINTER

One of the most expensive computer costs is printer cartridges. So, before you buy that cheap printer check to see how much the cartridges are and how often you're likely to have to replace them. It's worth spending a bit more money on a printer that has lower running costs.

785 REFILL FREELY

You can usually get printer cartridges refilled cheaper than you can buy new ones, and there are many specialist companies who will now do this for a very reasonable fee. Try to find a local cartridge-refilling store rather than buying new ones every time. Or refill them yourself if you're up to the challenge!

796 LIMIT YOUR GAMES

Online games can be major time and money pits, so look very carefully at your online games spending and limit yourself to an affordable number (or limit the hours you spend playing them). Keep an eye on your spending each month and stop once you reach your limit.

797 BUY SECOND-HAND CONSOLES

If you can't afford the latest gaming console, consider buying a second-hand version. Many gaming consoles, such as Playstation and Xbox, are updated regularly so there are lots of older models on the market. Check online at eBay and other shopping sites as well as on Amazon for used versions.

798 CASHBACK

If you are an avid hobby-gamer, see if you can turn your habit into a moneymaking opportunity. For instance, if you love Second Life, can you make enough inside to make some money on the outside? If so, you can offset your membership costs and even some other online costs.

799 DITCH THE MODEM

If you're paying for cable Internet, you don't have to use the modem the cable company gives you, which they are charging you rent for. You can pick up a cheap cable modem at most stores and after a year you're likely to have saved your modem rental costs.

800 GO ANNUAL

If you buy annual subscriptions or lifetime subscriptions instead of monthly for services you use regularly and believe will last three years or more, you could save yourself a whole chunk of money. Many online costs could be reduced by as much as 40 per cent by doing it this way, so it's worth investigating.

801 READ AN E-BOOK

Instead of buying a paper copy of a book, consider buying online instead. You have to get used to reading on the screen, but once you do (especially if you have a Tablet PC where the screens are built for e-reading) you could benefit greatly from reduced prices.

802 BENEFIT FROM A UPS

A proven method of shortening the life of your computers and electronics is to plug them directly into the wall. The use of a good-quality UPS not only gives you some much needed surge protection, you won't be subject to brownouts so your repair bills will come down.

803 GROUND YOURSELF

Use anti-static mats or ground yourself before touching your computer. Static electricity kills electronics, so try to make sure you're not wearing down your computer without knowing it. If you tend to get static shocks, you need to take action to prevent damage to your PC.

804 KEEP IT DUST-FREE

A sure-fire way to help your computer work more efficiently, and to reduce your possible future repair bills, is to keep your computer dust-free. Always make sure that you dust and wipe the back and top of your hard drive regularly. If you have space, you could use a dust cover.

805 KEEP A LIST

Keep a running list of online subscriptions and the time you spend using them. If you haven't logged in for weeks or months, do you really need to spend that money?

trips & holidays

806 SAVE IN ADVANCE

Try saving 10–15 per cent of your income for your holiday (vacation). Save for six months for one break mid-year or save all year round and have two breaks.

807 DON'T BE A SINGLE

Travelling alone can be expensive, with many hotels charging singles the same price as a couple especially during the school holidays. Luckily, specialist solo travel companies have begun to spring up offering deals for solo travellers. An alternative is to opt for a group tour and see it as a way to meet new people.

808 BE A COUCHSURFER

Couchsurfing is a way to stay for a very low price in other people's houses around the world. Not only do you get a free (or nearly free) night's sleep, you are also likely to get the sort of local knowledge that guidebooks can't give you. However, take into consideration your safety and make your arrangements through an established organization like www.couchsurfing.com or www.hospitalityclub.org.

809 STAY AT HOME

Don't just stay in your own country, actually stay in your own home. The cost of hiring a maid service, eating out every night and spending a couple of days in luxury could still be cheaper than heading overseas.

810 BUY IN ADVANCE

The best way to get holidays (vacations) cheaply is not only to save ahead, but to buy ahead too. It takes some forward planning, but the savings are likely to be immense. Booking a year ahead yields even better deals.

811 GO OFF-SEASON

If a destination has its highest tourist traffic in summer, plan your visit outside that time. It will be cheaper, you'll experience more local colour and you won't be annoyed by other tourists. However, it is important to check things like climate and weather conditions, as you do not want to arrive somewhere and discover that it is hurricane season!

812 CHECK YOUR DEAL

If your travel agent is offering you a deal you don't have to say 'yes' there and then. Ask how long they can keep it open, then check online to see if you can find it cheaper elsewhere. Agents are middlemen and have to make their money somehow, so see if you can bypass them for a saving.

813 TRUTHFUL BUDGETING

Budget for your cash spend while you're away and use your travel agent or the Internet to research options. Most importantly, be honest so that your budget is realistic. Give yourself a daily allowance to spend and stick to it.

814 PUT YOUR CARD AWAY

If you're going overseas, it's worth taking a credit card to use in emergencies, but make sure you only use it if you absolutely have to. Leave it in a safety deposit box to stop you from using it for normal holiday (vacation) spending.

815 AGENTS WORTH A TRY

Don't dismiss using travel agents as they can sometimes obtain better deals because of the volume discounts they get from providers. It's worth checking out what they can offer in case they have special deals that you won't find online.

816 BUY TRAVEL ONLINE

Use travel auction sites to help you travel like the rich and famous on a very meagre budget. Auction sites offer long-haul travel and luxury breaks at a fraction of the cost of travel agents, but make sure you do your research beforehand and always check the small print.

817 CRUISE LAST MINUTE

If you've got your heart set on a cruise, it's worth waiting until the last minute to book if you can be flexible, as they are often desperate to fill empty berths. Register for the e-mail alerts programme and you will be sent details of special offers.

818 CAMP OUT FOR A CHEAP HOLIDAY

Staying at a campsite can save you a lot of money. Many sites now have plenty of modern conveniences, which make for a less stressful stay, particularly if you're travelling with a family. If you prefer life on the wilder side, check out the local area in advance for places to stay in the wilderness.

819 SWAP YOUR HOME

If you want to travel abroad, but can't afford to pay for accommodation, why not do a house swap? You find someone who wants to stay in your house and you go to stay in theirs. There are organizations that will put you in touch with people. All you pay for is travel and subsistence while you're away. You have to be OK with someone living in your house for a week or two though.

820 YOU'LL BE GOOD WITH A B&B

Instead of staying in a hotel, try a bed and breakfast for a cheaper option. Many offer excellent facilities and a homely environment, and they often provide dinner for a fraction of the price of hotel meal. Things to check for are bathroom facilities and evening curfews.

821 HOTEL DIRECT

Booking directly with a hotel, especially if you're looking for a budget deal, is a good idea because you might get a better room. Hotels have 'categories' of rooms and are likely to save the worst rooms for budget deals, whereas their direct customers are likely to get something a little better.

822 SHOULDER THE FLIGHT

Travelling in the 'shoulder' period just before and after the school holidays is a great way to get your holiday (vacation) on a budget. Not only will the flights and hotels be cheaper, but the rental car and other expenses are also likely to fall.

823 GO OFF THE BEATEN TRACK

Take advantage of countries who, for whatever reason, are trying to boost their tourist credentials as you will often get great deals. However, there may be good reasons as to why people aren't travelling to certain places, so check with the relevant authority and make sure you do your research first.

824 HOMETOWN TOURIST

Why not try being a tourist in your hometown? Check out local websites and information, grab your camera and spend a few days exploring. You'll be amazed at the amount of things you walk straight past every day in your normal life, and it's a great way to relax on a budget.

825 WORK AWAY

Why not get paid to take a trip? Become an au pair, do seasonal work like picking fruit, or offer your teaching services or other skills. Investigate before you set off so that you can plan ahead.

826 VISIT A HOSTEL

Many hostels now have double rooms in addition to dormitory accommodation, so they can be good choices for friends travelling on a budget. Be sure to book ahead.

827 ROAD TRIP EXPENSES

If your holiday entails long stretches of driving, make sure you pack food before you go. This way you will avoid spending at restaurants, as well as the aggravation of trying to find a suitable place and time to stop. With your own food you can just pull over into a park or a place with a view to eat.

828 RENT AWAY

Renting an apartment, house, cottage or villa is usually far less expensive than staying in a hotel. It's a great way to cut down on food costs too as you usually cater for yourself. It doesn't mean you have to eat in every night, but going out every other night could cut your food costs substantially.

829 BARGAIN CALL

If a hotel is run independently or is part of a regional chain, don't be afraid to bargain with them to see what extras they can offer. Say something like, 'I already have a reservation at another hotel at a cheaper rate, but I'll book with you if I can get a third night free.'

air, car & rail travel

830 GET AIR MILES

Use credit cards, store cards, to rack up Air Miles that can be used to buy flights. Compare credit card deals carefully to make sure you're getting as many miles as possible.

831 BE FLEXIBLE

If you can, be flexible about which airport you fly from and to. Sometimes, it's cheaper to travel to a city's secondary airport, but do remember to include the cost of any extra travel you might have to do.

832 FLY OR DRIVE?

Before you decide to drive somewhere work out the costs of petrol (gasoline), wear and tear on your car, overnight stays, and so on. Airlines can often get you somewhere, especially if it's more than a few hours drive, cheaper and faster.

833 GET IN EARLY

Airlines can usually rely on business travellers booking at the last minute and pay top prices for flights, so by booking early you're making sure you get the best deal. This is especially good if you have set dates for flying – an event to attend, for example, where you can't be flexible.

834 BE A FREQUENT FLYER

Whether you fly for business or pleasure, becoming a member of a frequent flyer programme is a great idea as it lets you collect 'loyalty' points to redeem against upgrades, merchandise and hotel accommodation. It's particularly good for business clients because they tend not to mind being bound to one provider.

835 USE A DEBIT CARD

Using a debit card is a good way to reduce the cost of your flight as often there is a credit card fee, which can be up to 3 per cent. However, using a credit card is safer when it comes to getting your money back if anything goes wrong (if the airline goes out of business, for example) as debit card customers have less consumer protection.

836 BE ALERT

If you can be flexible about when you fly, why not sign up to airline websites and receive their e-mail alerts? Often, they sell off tickets in the low season, but make sure you take into account the final price, including surcharges, taxes, etc.

837 TRAVEL AT WEEKENDS

Travelling at weekends is a great way to make sure you get the lower-cost flights and train tickets, as they save their high prices for midweek business travellers. If you don't mind, fly at antisocial hours. These flights are less popular and therefore more likely to be discounted.

838 STAY SATURDAY

When you take a break, try to stay Saturday night. That way, the airline's system won't think you're a wealthy business customer and charge you more. The same goes for weekday travel – try not to travel on Monday morning or Friday night when prices are likely to be higher.

839 OFFER TO BUMP

This one could actually make you money! If you can be flexible, tell your airline you don't mind being 'bumped'. This will mean that you are volunteering to fly later in the event that the plane is oversubscribed (there are too many people and not enough seats). They are often so glad to have volunteers that they will pay you for your trouble.

840 TRY FOR EXTRAS

When you check in, see if you can get a bit of extra room. Upgrades are usually reserved for members of frequent flyer programmes or loyalty card holders, but if you dress smartly, ask politely and cross your fingers, you might get it!

841 RECLAIM TAX

Did you know that you can reclaim your air passenger duty (part of the ticket cost) if you cancel an airline ticket? Some airlines impose a charge for this that can be almost as much as the claim, but for long-haul flights it's almost always worth it.

842 WATCH YOUR OPTIONS

Make sure the cost of your cheap flight doesn't rack up with 'optional' charges like checking you in and charging for food. Be clear about what you're buying before you commit and make plans to minimize extra costs, such as checking in online, travelling with hand luggage, having a meal onboard or buying headphones for inflight entertainment.

843 BUY DOUBLE

As ridiculous as it sounds, a return (round-trip) ticket usually costs less than a single (one way). Think creatively to solve the problem – sometimes, buying two return (round-trip) airfares and using just one half of each is actually cheaper than buying two singles (one-way tickets).

844 ROUND THE WORLD

If you're travelling on long-haul flights, particularly for an extended period, it's worth checking out specialist round-the-world ticket providers. They can often get you better deals than the airlines because of their flexibility.

845 SLEEP ON THE MOVE

Save the cost of a night in a hotel and airport transfers by taking a sleeper train between major cities. Sleeping on the train means you arrive refreshed, the train is likely to be quiet and you'll have saved a heap of money.

846 COLLISION DANGER

If you rent a car, the likelihood is you'll be cautioned about the need to buy an optional collision-damage waiver. Check your own car insurance policy first though because you may already be covered. If not, then pay with a credit card, which should cover you for most car rentals. Always read the small print carefully though, so you don't get caught out.

847 CONSIDER THE TRAIN

Trains can be a cheap and comfortable option for travelling around a country once you get there. Most countries have good, reliable train networks, including the UK, India, South Africa, USA, Canada, Australia and New Zealand. You can book tickets through www.Seat61.com that covers most destinations.

848 DRIVE FOR FREE

If you are over 25 and want to drive across America, why not deliver a car? For the price of your petrol (gasoline) and a deposit, you can drive someone elses car across the country. Be careful though, check the route as you are likely to have to follow a set of directions that might not include the places you want to visit.

849 BAG A BARGAIN

Most flights leave the ground with about 20 per cent of the seats unsold, so make sure you take advantage of last-minute deals where you can. The later you can leave it, the better the deal you can get.

cheap dates & days out

850 GET OUT FOR FREE

Pick up a local newspaper and check upcoming free events. There are often concerts, arts and crafts fairs, plays, festivals, art galleries and museums that offer entertainment for free or for very little, so keep an eye on what's going on.

851 MAKE A DATE AT HOME

You don't have to eat out to have a romantic dinner. Just have a date night at home for a fraction of the cost. Use your best china and cutlery, open a bottle of wine, light some candles and serve a special meal, such as steak. It will still be far cheaper than going out.

852 ROMANTIC READING

One of the cheapest, but most romantic dates is the simplest: take turns reading poetry or a novel to each other in bed.

853 TASTE WINE FOR FREE

Even if you don't live near a famous wine region, such as Napa valley in California or Bordeaux in France, your local winery or wine school may host free wine tastings. If you can, go on weekdays when the pouring is more generous and the venue less crowded. Some establishments are now charging for tastings, but even so these are great value for money and lots of fun. If your local winery doesn't hold free tastings, try your off-license (liquor store); many of these offer samplings at set times of the week.

854 BOOKSTORE AND COFFEE-SHOP EVENTS

These venues often sponsor lectures, live music and book readings and signings – in which case you might be in for a free glass of wine and canapés.

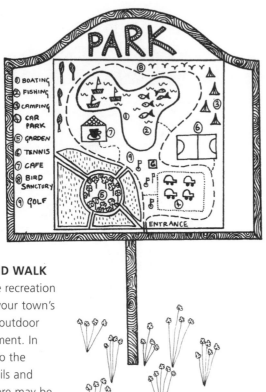

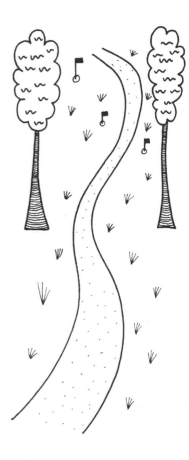

855 PARK AND WALK

Check the recreation board in your town's parks for outdoor entertainment. In addition to the nature trails and walks, there may be free tennis courts, sports grounds and activities to take advantage of.

856 CHECK OUT CHURCHES, SCHOOLS AND COLLEGES

It might not be the New York Met or the Royal Opera House, but there are plenty of free concerts and theatre performances at churches and schools. Many also sponsor auctions, raffles, fetes and fairs, barbecues and other fund-raising events that are entertaining and good for bargain-hunting.

857 SEE THE STARS

The stars and planets feature in many famous love stories, from the star-crossed lovers Romeo and Juliet to the moon in *It's a Wonderful Life*. For a romantic afternoon or evening date, take a trip to a planetarium or observatory to connect your love to the mysteries of the universe.

858 MOVIE MARATHON

For sci-fi fans, rent the full set of *Star Wars* or *The Lord of the Rings* trilogy. For romantics, rent oldies but goodies, such as *Casablanca*, *Roman Holiday* and *An Affair to Remember*. Make some popcorn and relax for a night's viewing.

859 WORK WITH YOUR AREA

If you live in a coastal area, take advantage of the water to surf, dive, water-ski or snorkel; if you live in a snowy region, go sledding or ice-skating; go yachting or rowing on nearby rivers; and in the mountains take advantage of nature trails and parkland. Even going off-season can be fun – try flying a kite or collecting shells at the beach in the winter, for example.

860 PRETEND YOUR GARDEN IS THE CARIBBEAN

If you can't afford to get away, stay at home and take advantage of a hot summer's day by pretending your backyard is a beach paradise. Set up a sun lounger and sit out with a good book, your sunglasses and suncream. If you have a pool or water feature, all the better; if not, make do with a lawn water sprinkler. The idea of the artificial beach has been taken up by cities across the globe – such as the Paris-Plage along the Seine in Paris – as welcome relief to urban-dwellers during the summer months.

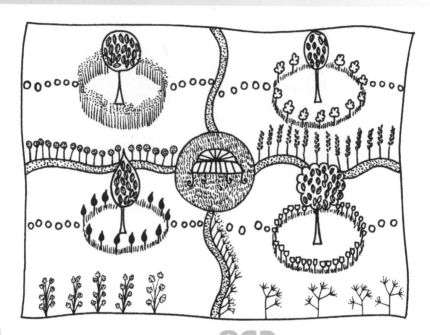

861 GARDEN STATE

Botanical gardens and horticultural centres offer a beautiful space in which to have long scenic walks in the outdoors. Many have a range of different gardens, such as herb, physic or rainforest, as well as extra exhibitions, concerts and shows. There are sometimes conservatories and hothouses for inside viewing, too.

862 AL FRESCO FUN

Outdoor picnics can work well in many locations – parks, the beach, forests or any picturesque location. They are even better when combined with an activity, such as swimming, boating or listening to a free concert. Alternatively set up an indoor picnic or midnight feast with tea-lights, background music and soft blankets.

863 BE A TRAILFINDER

Rambling, hiking, cycling and other
cross-country activities in national parks,
forests and open countryside are available
for free to everyone. Many organizations,
such as hiking and ramblers clubs, offer
advice on established trails and encourage
participation in educational exhibits, trail-
clearing and projects.

864 GET YOUR SKATES ON

Rollerblading, rollerskating and ice-skating
are all fun, inexpensive date ideas that
are guaranteed to break the ice. Old-
school roller-skating rinks playing classic
oldie music is nostalgic fun, or if you're
the athletic type all you need are your
rollerblades and a city park.

865 GAME NIGHT

Dig out your family board games or
download a free trivia quiz from the
Internet for a quiz night in your own home.
Make it more challenging by playing for
stakes – perhaps the loser gets to wash the
dishes or clean the car.

866 RADIO STATION GIVEAWAYS

Call in to your local radio station to try
and win free concert tickets. If you win,
your date will think you've really splashed
out, but if you aren't lucky, radio stations
sometimes run free concerts by little-
known bands so keep an ear out for these.

867 GO TO GALLERY OPEN DAYS

Art galleries can offer much more than just their permanent collections, such as films, concerts, lectures and special exhibitions. Try your local art galleries and auction houses, too. Many art areas in towns and cities sponsor open mornings where you can visit a range of galleries and enjoy drinks and nibbles while you view.

868 HISTORIC HOMES AND MUSEUMS

Keep track of events at historic stately homes or mansions in your area as they may have cut-price tickets, special promotions tied to their anniversary dates or Christmas or public holiday activities. Also check your local historic preservation society for any upcoming events that might be open to the public.

getting married

869 SEND A PRINT

Make your own inexpensive thank-you cards by using a wedding photograph as a postcard. Simply print the image on to thick paper or card, write on the back and send.

870 BUY SECOND-HAND

A second-hand wedding dress doesn't have to fit you perfectly. Alterations are usually quite simple if you find a good seamstress or alteration service, and many bridal stores can also do this for you. Choose a dress that is a size too big to allow for proper fitting.

871 DONATION REQUEST

Instead of having a wedding gift list, you could always ask guests for a donation towards something big, like a new bed a car or even your honeymoon. People want to give wedding gifts to help you in your future life together, so be honest about what you need.

872 GO MODERN

Increasingly, brides-to-be are choosing outfits for their wedding day that can be worn again. Consider an evening dress (you can always have it shortened and dyed later if you don't go to many evening functions) or separates and trouser-suits.

873 PRINT YOUR OWN

Instead of spending lots of money ordering printed stationery, do it yourself on your computer or see if you can take advantage of discounts through the company you work for. If you have to use professional printers you can lower the cost by doing the design yourself.

874 ASK FOR AN UPGRADE

If you are going somewhere on your honeymoon, make sure you ask for specials and free upgrades wherever you go and inform hotels and other venues before you arrive that you're honeymooning as they will often leave free hampers, bottles of champagne or fruit baskets in your room as a gift.

875 USE YOUR FRIENDS

A great way to lower costs at a wedding
is to use the skills of your friends and
family – one of your friends might be
gifted enough to make your wedding
cake! Flower arranging, decorating and
photography are other obvious options
(ask for them as wedding gifts) and hair,
make-up and even dressmaking are great
ideas, too.

876 BUY IN THE SALES

If you're buying your bridesmaid's dresses,
don't limit yourself to looking in bridal
stores, where prices are often sky-high.
Look in the eveningwear sections of
department stores and other outlets and
try to buy in the sales to minimize costs.
Alternatively try dress-hire stores, who sell
off last season's clothes at bargain prices.

877 MAKE CONFETTI SUBSTITUTES

Instead of buying confetti, make your
own – cut up bits of tissue, spray-paint
rice, dry flower petals on a very low heat
in the oven or use bubbles instead.

878 MAKE A LIST

Department stores sometimes offer incentives to have your gift list with them, even if people don't end up using it. You simply have to sign up, then even if you don't use the list you've made with them, you'll often get a free voucher to spend.

879 USE A STUDENT

A professional photographer is often one of the most expensive elements of a wedding day. Ask around at local colleges for students who have recently graduated from photography courses or final-year students, who will usually do it for a small fee. Make sure you are clear about what you want from them, as they will be inexperienced.

880 NOT NECESSARILY NEW

Don't always think you have to buy a new engagement or wedding ring. There are many second-hand jewellery stores that sell used (or sometimes ordered, but not picked up) rings. You can have rings altered or even use the stones in another setting, so explore your options before you buy new.

881 MAKE A GOWN

Don't throw away your wedding dress or keep it in the attic gathering dust. Unless you want to keep it for your own daughter's wedding, why not make use of it for a child's christening gown, have it altered or dyed to create a cocktail dress or corset and skirt, or use the silk from the train or skirt to make cushions (pillows).

882 CHANGE THE DAY

If you get married on a Thursday, Friday or Sunday and you can almost halve the cost – and you're more likely to get everything you want rather than it being booked up. Choose low season for the best deals.

883 SELL IT

Why not sell your wedding dress or outfit on eBay? You could even ask for your bridesmaids' dresses back at the end of the day and sell them as a job lot or as separate items. There is a roaring trade in second-hand wedding dresses as women are increasingly less willing to spend a month's earnings on something they're only going to wear once.

884 PRIORITIZE YOUR SPENDING

The most important thing when planning wedding spending is to prioritize. Sit down with your fiancé and go through the list of expenses deciding where you want to concentrate costs and where you can make savings. For example, you might be willing to forego professional photographs if it means guests don't have to pay for booze.

885 CREATIVE TABLE DECORATIONS

Instead of buying lots of fresh flowers for your table decorations, why not use small plants instead? You can give them to guests to take home afterwards. Another idea is to fill glass bowls or vases with found items such as twigs, pine cones and moss (you can always spray-paint the items to match your colour scheme).

886 DISPOSABLE IMAGES

Instead of paying a photographer to stay around into the evening, why not put disposable cameras on the tables and ask guests to take photos? They then leave the cameras in a bag or basket that you have put by the door on their way home. Alternatively, make a point of asking guests to take photos with their own digital cameras and to e-mail them to you or upload them to a special page online.

celebrations

887 SET A BUDGET

Whenever you've got to buy a gift, and whoever you have to buy it for, set a budget. It's no use buying that 'perfect' gift for a friend or relative if it's going to mean you can't pay your bills at the end of the month. The earlier you have an idea of your budget, the sooner you can start being creative or searching for the ideal gift.

888 TAKE A LONG VIEW

If you have a younger friend, sister or god-daughter to buy for, gifts that you can add to over the years are a great choice. Give a pearl a year, for instance, and they'll have a necklace by the time they want to wear it, or a charm bracelet with one charm every birthday.

889 GIVE YOUR TIME

If a friend or family member has just had a new baby, the thing they are likely to be most in need of is a little time to relax. Instead of buying a gift, offer to clean their house or cook a meal once a week so they can get a bit of well-earned rest.

890 BUY A BIBLE

An inexpensive, yet thoughtful christening present is a Bible. Add to it by making your own bookmark with some thoughtful passages or writing a personalized note. You could wrap it in a newspaper from the day of the christening.

891 SAVE ON PARTY ESSENTIALS

Go to your local discount store for small items such as candles, streamers, balloons and other party items, and recycle items from year to year to save money. Themes for Easter, Christmas, Thanksgiving, Diwali and other celebrations never change so this is a good way to celebrate special occasions on a budget.

892 BUY TO LAST

Instead of spending lots of money on traditional silver gifts for a christening, why not look to the future? Speak to a local wine merchant for advice on wines and ports that will mature well and buy a (probably inexpensive) bottle now that will be a fantastic (and expensive) bottle by the time the child is legally allowed to drink it.

893 WRITE A POEM

A great gift for a special occasion if you're short on cash is to write a poem. Write using a calligraphy pen or special ink and present it in a frame (bought or recycled) or roll it up like a scroll to make it really special. Plunder anthologies of poems until you find one you like, or look in editions dedicated to themes of love or friendship. Alternatively, use lyrics from one of the songs by your favourite musicians.

894 HELP AT HALLOWEEN

Buy next year's costumes for 50 per cent discount the week following Halloween. Alternatively, revamp existing costumes and add accessories to make them a little different rather than buying a whole new outfit – a red cape could be use for Dracula, Red Riding Hood, the Devil or Superman while angels, princesses, fairies and brides are all interchangeable.

895 MAKE YOUR OWN CHOCOLATES

Instead of buying expensive Belgian chocolates for a birthday or dinner-party gift, make your own chocolates or fudge. These are also great to offer at holiday times, for Easter or after dinner, and can stand on their own as a special dessert. For Easter chocolates, make your own chocolate eggs using cheap plastic moulds or make up an Easter basket with an assortment of homemade and purchased goodies.

throwing a party

896 BE A MAGPIE

Make a point of always being on the lookout for items that you can buy to put into your children's fancy dress (costume) box. It's likely they will go to a few dress-up parties during a year so look out for giveaways and second-hand bargains. Hats are a good option as they last for years.

897 PERSONAL GIFT VOUCHERS

Next time you have to buy a gift for someone but are strapped for cash, give them a book of 'service' vouchers from you that they can redeem. Include ideas like gardening, a massage, manicure or pedicure, handwashing clothes, ironing – anything that will make their life easier.

898 INVITE THEM OVER

Instead of giving expensive gifts and paying a lot of money to go out to eat with friends on their birthday, why not prepare a meal at your home for them? Invite a few mutual friends and make something they love. Even if everyone brings a bottle, you'll all still save on restaurant costs.

899 SERVE A SHOT

If you're having a big dinner party and want to serve after-dinner liqueurs but don't have enough shot glasses, make up your own chocolate shot glasses. Line a shot glass with cling film (plastic wrap) and paint layers of melted chocolate on the inside (allow each layer to dry) until you have a thick enough 'glass' to hold. Lift out the chocolate 'glass' and refrigerate until use. The chocolate can be eaten after the contents have been drunk.

900 THINK OF A THEME

Why not theme your party and make it a fancy dress (costume) night? You'll have to spend less on the decorations because everyone's costumes will be colourful enough and you can be inventive around your theme, which could be anything from decades and events to things like heroes and villains, which allow guests to put their own spin on the idea.

901 ACCEPT ALL OFFERS

When entertaining, if one of your guests offers to bring food, take them up on it. Also, there's absolutely nothing wrong with a 'bring your own booze' invitation, particularly if you're providing food. That way everyone will bring what they like and you won't overspend by trying to cater for everyone's tastes.

902 PUNCH YOUR WEIGHT

A great choice for a budget party drink is a punch. Use fruit juice as a base (buy pasteurized rather than fresh as it's cheaper), then add lemonade (Sprite/7UP) or ginger ale and some vodka or rum if you want to add an extra zing. Try mixing fruit flavours like orange and pineapple or cranberry and apple for the base.

903 THEME OF THE YEAR

For parties to celebrate a landmark birthday, why not have a party themed on the year of the person's birth? You can use the same idea for anniversaries, which can be themed around the year the wedding took place.

904 THE JOY OF SINGING

Karaoke forms a great centrepiece for a budget party as once you've bought, borrowed or hired the machine it's a free night's entertainment for everyone. You could ask your guests to dress up as their favourite music star.

905 BUDGET AND STICK TO IT

The first step when you're party planning is to decide what your budget is and stick to it. Use your own home as a (free) venue or choose somewhere inexpensive like a park, church hall or sports club. Try to make the food yourself or ask friends to bring a dish (as long as you coordinate to avoid having ten salads and no dessert!).

906 GO LARGE

While small bottles and packages of things might look cuter at your party, the best way to save money on feeding and watering your guests is to buy in bulk. Use large bottles of juices and drinks, put water in jugs and buy cases of beer and wine (as long as you're not overbuying) to minimize costs.

907 PLAN TO ENTERTAIN

Whether you're organizing an adults' or kid's party, you need to think about the entertainment. A successful party needs to be 'built' around a centrepiece – whether it's music and a dance floor, a quiz or a series of organized games.

908 KEEP A CHECK

Making a checklist will allow you to see how far you have progressed in your party planning, what needs to be done and, most importantly, whether you are on budget. This will keep you focused and also give you enough time to see if you are missing something or not.

909 DELEGATE, DELEGATE, DELEGATE

The chances of you being able to organize a budget party on your own are very slim. Ask friends for help, delegate responsibility to others or start a 'party club' with a group of neighbours or friends where you agree to help each other with a certain number of parties each year. Even asking everyone to bring a dish helps enormously.

children's parties

910 INTIMATE GATHERINGS

Children don't need a large birthday party every year. They could just choose one or two friends and you can take them out for an activity such as swimming or bowling, or to a movie, the theatre or to a fun restaurant.

911 JEWELLED CREATIONS

Your children's party guests can make their own edible take-home jewellery. Buy sweets (candy), chocolates, dried fruits and marshmallows and the children can string them onto long strips of liquorice to make edible necklaces or bracelets.

912 HAVE A FILM NIGHT

A movie-themed birthday celebration is a great idea for an older child. Help the kids make their own popcorn, pizzas or fajitas, then let them snuggle up in front of a DVD, play film quizzes or set them a film-themed treasure hunt around the garden or local park.

913 GET CRAFTY

For a great, cheap children's craft party make your own playdough with 1 cup plain (all-purpose) flour, ½ cup salt, 2 tablespoons cream of tartar and 1 cup of water with food colouring. Heat in a saucepan or microwave until it forms a ball, knead and store in an airtight container. If it goes hard, add a teaspoon of oil, reheat and it's as good as new.

914 BUDGET BIRTHDAY CAKE

A great way to make your own spectacular budget birthday cake is to buy a cheap iced (frosted) cake from a budget store and use coloured icing or icing pens to model or draw on your own design. Scour the many Internet sites dedicated to cake decorating for ideas and adapt it to your own theme.

915 LET THEM MAKE THEIR OWN

Instead of spending lots of money on party bags, organize an activity so that the children make their own gift. Decorating cupcakes or gingerbread, making a fun animal mask or painting a plant pot are all great, cheap ideas. Alternatively, set up a treasure hunt and each child can search for their gift.

916 MAKE A PIÑATA

A piñata is a brightly coloured paper container filled with gifts like small toys and sweets (candy). You hang it from a tree or hook in the ceiling and the children take turns being blindfolded and hitting it with a stick until it breaks open and spills the prizes.

917 KEEP OLDER KIDS HAPPY

If you're planning a party for older children, try to make your party-gift craft projects a bit more grown up. Tie-dying T-shirts or throws, threading jewellery or using seashells and beads to decorate photo frames or mirrors are all great girly ideas; for boys, woodworking, making their own pizza or creating paper planes are good suggestions.

christmas

918 BE A SECRET SANTA

Secret Santa is where a group of people agree to buy one present each of the same monetary value to give to someone specific whose name is drawn out of a hat, but the recipient does not know who the gift is from. The great thing about it is if there are lots of people to buy for – large families, school classes and colleagues – it means you only have to buy one gift.

918 STOCK YOUR CUPBOARD

Set aside one cupboard in your kitchen and designate it the 'Christmas cupboard'. Make a list of all the food you need to buy for the celebration, then (making sure you check the use by dates) buy something every few weeks to spread the cost of stocking the cupboard. This idea can be used for any big celebration where you need to buy lots of food.

920 CARRY A LIST

If you're going to start buying gifts for Christmas in January and carry on throughout the year, it's important you stay organized to avoid forgetting what you've bought and wasting money. Carry a list of what you've bought and who for.

921 SAVE YOUR VOUCHERS

Make a decision to help save money next Christmas – save up your vouchers, coupons or reward points throughout the year to spend on your Christmas shopping, or use them throughout the year if they are dated to build your preparations.

922 FESTIVE SAVINGS

There's no reason to get into debt because of Christmas – it comes around at the same time every year, so there's no surprise. If you find yourself struggling, start preparing early by putting some money away each month or buying a few bits here and there to spread the cost.

923 HOMEMADE CHEER

Instead of buying Christmas decorations to make your house feel festive for the holiday season, make your own. Create old-fashioned paper chains using angel, tree or holly-leaf shapes or make snowflakes by folding and cutting paper and hang around in clusters or garlands.

924 SAVE UP

If you are worried that you won't have the willpower to save up for Christmas all year round, why not join a credit union or Christmas savings club? This will help you to put away a certain amount of money in a safe place until the festive season. Join early in the year for the best savings.

925 GET SALE SAVVY

Christmas decorations and gifts are usually half price or less in the post-Christmas (January) sales, so make sure you take advantage and stock up then. Buy anything from wrapping paper, ribbons and napkins to candles, ornaments and lights.

926 MAKE A HAMPER

Visit the local farmer's market to make up a great Christmas hamper to give as a present. If that's too pricey, use a few items from the market and then fill it up with generic supermarket items like crackers and so on.

927 CHIP IN

Instead of bearing the brunt of your Christmas buying alone, try to find people to chip in with. Sharing the cost of mum and dad's present with a sibling, for instance, means you can get a better gift for less and you'll benefit from each other's ideas too.

928 BRANCH OUT

Instead of paying money for a Christmas tree, use a branch from someone's pine tree (ask friends and family to wait till winter to cut trees back, for instance) or use dropped branches you find in the park or from your garden. Spray the branches silver or green for an arty look or leave woody and add lights and baubles.

929 TAKE A BREAK

Have you thought about taking a holiday (vacation) instead of holding a traditional and expensive Christmas celebration? Agree to forego the presents and head off to the sun or ski slopes instead – you'll be amazed at what a great holiday (vacation) you can all afford if you cut your Christmas spending. Plus, because you'll be away for the holidays, you won't have to throw a party, send greetings cards or give gifts to everyone you might have otherwise.

having a baby

930 PARENT AND BABY TIME

Mother and baby groups run by churches are usually inexpensive and they give you the opportunity to meet other mothers and for your kids to play with other children. Groups such as these are much cheaper than paying lots of money for commercial children's entertainment activities.

931 BE PRACTICAL

If you're having a baby shower, ask for practical gifts such as clothes, bedding and toiletries. A great new idea is a 'nappy (diaper) cake', which looks like a tiered, wedding-style cake but it is made from lots of rolled nappies.

932 KNOW WHEN TO BUY USED

Buying a cot (crib) second-hand is a great idea, but second-hand mattresses are linked with increased sudden infant death syndrome and allergies, so do make sure you replace the mattress.

933 JOIN A LIBRARY

Joining a toy library is a great idea because it enables you to borrow toys for an average of two weeks for a really small fee. What this means is that you can try out lots of toys and if your kids really like something, then you can consider buying it.

934 SAFETY ON THE MOVE

Don't buy a second-hand child car seat unless you are absolutely certain it hasn't been involved in an accident, as this could weaken it and endanger your baby. However, accepting a hand-me-down from family or a friend that you can trust will save you a lot of money.

935 BUDGET ON CLOTHES

Try to avoid buying expensive baby clothes when the baby is newborn, as they will constantly be in the washing machine and will be too small in a matter of weeks. By the time your baby is a year old they will wear clothes for a little longer so you can start justifying a little more cash at this time.

936 BREAST IS CHEAPEST

Not only is breastfeeding better for your baby, it's a lot cheaper than formula. Even if you express and have to buy a few bottles, the cost is nothing compared to the bottles, sterilizer, formula powder and cleaning equipment you need for bottle-feeding.

937 MAKE A LIST

If there are a lot of things you need, but can't afford, consider making a baby gift list as you would a wedding gift list. Ask friends and family who are likely to buy you a present to buy something from the list. That way you get what you need without getting into debt.

938 GIVE ADVICE

If you've had a baby, you're in a great position to give a first-time mum an invaluable gift – your experience. Make them up an inexpensive hamper of baby essentials and include a book of mantras like 'I'm a great mother' and inspirational quotes, which they can refer to when things get hard. You could also include babysitting tokens to be redeemed throughout the first year.

streetwise shopping

939 EAT WELL

On the day of the sales, have a really good breakfast to ensure you have enough energy to survive the madness! If you really want to shop the sales seriously, it's important to get there reasonably early or all of the best items will be gone. But be prepared for some pushing and shoving – take water and snacks with you to keep you going and keep your mind on your target, don't get sidetracked.

940 CHECK THE SMALL PRINT

Always make sure at the time of purchase that you check what the store's return policy is. They all differ and for sale items the policies are often different to their normal ones. If you can get away with buying an item without trying it on, rather than waiting at a busy changing room, and then return it at a later date if it's not suitable, do it.

941 VOUCHER VALUE

If you are a member of a supermarket reward scheme, it's often better to use the vouchers to pay for magazine subscriptions, theatre vouchers or other entertainment tickets as they're worth more than when used in the store to redeem for cash. But be careful to only buy what you would have bought anyway, or you're not saving.

942 ASK AROUND

If the store doesn't have an item of clothing you want in your size, ask them to check the stockroom and call their other branches to see if one can be put on hold for you or sent to the store for pick-up. If the store is too busy to call for you, ask for the numbers and do it yourself.

943 WALK IT OUT

If you're sale shopping bear in mind that you can cover a vast distance in a day. Wear comfortable shoes so that your feet won't get sore and choose a style that you can slip on and off to try on other shoes – ballet pumps or slip-on loafers are good choices.

944 HAGGLE IT DOWN

Even if you're shopping in chain stores, don't be afraid to haggle. If they can't give you a discount on the price, they can always throw in extras like extra cables for a laptop or batteries for a toy or game. Don't be afraid to ask.

945 MAKE A BEELINE

If you're heading out to the sales, spend a day doing your research beforehand. Go to your favourite stores and ask them what is likely to be on sale, make a note of items you love and would like to get for discount and even try them on so you know what size to aim for come sale day.

946 KNOW YOUR CYCLE

If you have favourite stores, keep an eye on their merchandise cycle – this is the amount of time the clothes spend out on the store floor before they are replaced or discounted. If you know the cycles, you can better take advantage of outlet discounts and reduced prices.

947 TIME IT RIGHT

If you're buying a big Christmas gift, such as a TV or digital camera, why not write an IOU for the product and give that to the person on the day? Then promise to buy it after Christmas when it's reduced in the sales (or spend the same money and get a better version).

car-boot (garage) sales & markets

948 BE FIRM

When someone asks you a price for something you're selling, answer them firmly. If you say something like 'I was thinking…' or 'is XX OK?', chances are they will haggle. Buyers are more likely to part with their money if you don't have price labels, as it gives them a chance to haggle you down. Start a little higher than the price you would take (but only a little) and give them the satisfaction.

949 TAKE CASH

There's no point taking credit cards and other valuables to the sale. Take what you can safely carry and leave the rest at home – any held in car parks (parking lots) are notoriously good picking grounds for thieves, so try to keep everything on you. Take plenty of loose change and notes, and only take the amount you are willing to spend – that way, you won't get carried away in the excitement.

950 **TEST YOUR KNOWLEDGE**

Before you go to a car-boot (garage) sale or flea market, buy a local paper to find out when and where the sale is, check online, look for ads in the local area or simply ask around. Be prepared to get there early if you want to find the bargains. Very early.

951 PACK IT AWAY

Take lots of carrying bags, a shopping trolley (cart) or backpack if you have one. Even use a child's pram (baby-carriage) or other wheelable device. You'll be amazed how heavy those little items are when you have to carry them around all day, and if you're resting you aren't getting bargains!

952 LOOK AROUND

Have a good look on, under, around and past the seller's table, because some of the more interesting or special items may be kept safe so they don't get harmed. Ask the seller if they've got anything else on offer and be prepared to walk around a second time as new merchandise emerges as tables become emptier.

953 LEAVE PAPER ALONE

If you're buying paper items, make extra sure they're not damaged as chances are they will have been out in the rain at previous sales at some point. Avoid envelopes, cigarette papers and other items that might be ruined by moisture.

954 GO ALONE

Don't go shopping with small children and animals. Leave them at home with someone to look after them and head out alone to bargain hunt, particularly in hot weather – there's nothing better to stop you haggling than a whingeing child or a panting dog.

955 BUY MULTIPLE

If you're buying more than one item from one seller, you can ask for a multiple-item discount, but make sure you don't add extra items just to get a discount, as that's a false economy. You can always return later to see if the price has dropped, sellers often do this near the end of the day.

956 WALK THE LINE

At large sales and markets, individual stalls are usually laid out in a grid. To avoid missing possible bargains, try to plan your route – start at one end and work your way methodically through, doing first right- and then left-side stalls, or however you want to work it, but stick to your plan.

957 TURN THE TABLES

The best way to get rid of your items at a sale is to make sure people can see them – set them out on tables, have plastic sheeting ready to protect them if it rains and don't use hard-to-remove sticky price tags that might prevent buyers taking an item.

958 ARRANGE IT

Use logic to arrange your stall. Put similar items together, like cosmetics, pictures or CDs; keep DVDs, food items, perfumes and such on top of tables and consign less likely sales, such as cuddly toys and kitchen equipment, to the ground. Hang clothes on rails if you can, or take a rummage basket for larger items like curtains and blankets.

959 GET A BUDDY

It's always better to have two people running a stall at a sale. Not only will you have company, you can take it in turns to have toilet breaks, get drinks and food, and have a browse of the other stalls. And, it's much more fun.

960 TAKE CHANGE

Not all buyers will bring loose change with them, so make sure you have more than you need. You don't want to risk losing a sale because you can't offer someone the correct change for an item.

961 LOCK UP

For a car sale, keep your car doors locked when you are serving, and your takings somewhere safe to avoid being the victim of theft. If you're having a garage sale, make sure your house is secure and nobody can get into any area of your home where you don't want them.

962 HAVE A BARGAIN BIN

Why not copy the supermarkets and offer a 'buy one get one free' table or basket, or even a 'three for two'. It's a great way to get rid of things you really don't want and it means you can concentrate on selling the higher-value items. This is particularly good for small items like costume jewellery and bangles, CDs or DVDs, or any food items.

internet buying & selling

963 GET CASH BACK

Investigate the possibility of earning rebates while you shop online. There are a range of stores who offer money or vouchers in exchange for buying through their website. Only use this for things you would have bought anyway; don't be seduced by 'bargains' and 'cashback' rewards you don't need. Be aware though that 40 per cent of those eligible for rebates don't redeem them.

964 CHECK FEEDBACK

If you're buying on an Internet auction site, such as eBay, make sure you check the seller's reputation and feedback before you buy. If the feedback is poor, think twice about parting with your money. If you have any questions always ask them before bidding, particularly if order details such as who pays delivery cost, insurance costs and so on aren't clear.

965 BE SECURE

Be careful when you give your credit or debit card details on the Internet. Always find out whether the company has a secure site by looking for the closed padlock sign at the bottom of your computer screen, and look for information about the online protection the company has put in place. Most reputable firms will offer this freely.

966 READ THE TERMS

As tempting as it is to click on that 'I agree' box they put under the terms and conditions without actually reading it, make a habit of doing so. You wouldn't give money to a man on the street without agreeing terms, so don't do it online either.

967 CHECK SHIPPING

Before you agree to the purchase, check for high shipping costs or other hidden costs such handling and storage. If you're buying from abroad you'll also need to check out import taxes, which can be fairly high, and make sure you get an agreed delivery time. Calculate the total cost before you buy.

968 KNOW THE RETURNS POLICY

Most Internet companies have pretty good returns policies, but it's worth checking before you buy what the policy is on returning goods you don't like or want and, in particular, who will pay the return delivery costs. Especially bear this in mind when buying heavy items. If buying from abroad, check to see if there will be any additional customs tax.

969 PRINT IT OUT

Print out your order from the online site and check it matches with the confirmation e-mail you are sent. You should also keep a bookmark or printed copy of the terms and conditions page so you can refer back to it.

970 USE CREDIT

The best way to pay for items on the Internet is to use your credit card, which will offer you more protection than a debit card or money transfer. In the case of fraudulent sites, credit card payers usually get their money back first, so make sure you're one of them.

971 CONTACT DETAILS

If you are unsure about the seller's security credentials, look for an address and telephone number. Check out where they are based and if necessary do a search to see if you can find out more about them.

making money

972 SELL YOUR BODY

Aside from selling stuff you don't want any more, you can also be paid for participating in medical trials and, in some countries, for donations of blood plasma. Check out drug companies for medical trials or ask at your local medical centre for advice.

973 BE A READER

If you're a student, take advantage of your education to make a little extra cash. Offer tutorial services on your subject or on how to get a place in higher education, or proofread and edit essays and CVs (résumés).

974 SEARCH THE ATTIC

Take a good look through you and your family's attic and basement for any treasures that could be sold. Your aunt's collection of Elvis t-shirts or your dad's old vinyl collection could turn out to bring in quite a lot of cash if you sell it over the Internet (just ask them first!).

975 BE AN EXPERT

If you have a skill or are educated to a high level in something (think everything from French, mathematics and computer skills to plumbing, astrology and music), offer your services as a private tutor. It's a great way to make money doing something you enjoy.

976 THE PERKS OF THE JOB

It's worth looking at the most expensive things in your life, and things you don't want to compromise on, and seeing if there's a way to get a discount. Working in a restaurant or fast-food outlet, for example, should give you free food or a job in a clothing store will get you a discount.

977 WORK THE WEB

If you know about a subject, or have a group of friends you could do it with, set up a website. You can do it for very little cost on your home computer and if you score hits you could make some money out of AdSense or other advertising packages.

978 WRITE UP REVIEWS

If you have skills as a writer, you can sign up to review gigs, music, restaurants, films, or spas and beauty products for local newspapers and magazines or online websites. Not only will you get the experience for free, but you'll get a small sum for your review or article too.

979 STRIKE A POSE

If you are interested in fine art, you may be able to model for a life-study art class. For nude modelling you will be expected to remain fairly motionless except for moving poses, and instructors often prefer poses in which the body is being exerted for a more dynamically interesting subject. Many educational institutes hire art students, but always choose a reputable organization.

980 RENT OUT YOUR HOME

Film, television and advertising scouts are always on the lookout for locations for shooting. Your home doesn't have to be perfect – it might be just the ordinary interior they are looking for, or you might have desirable outdoor space. Using the interior as a location is usually more profitable than if just the external view is used. There are a number of online agencies that will list your property for free (only taking commission once your property is chosen for a shoot). Always avoid any that charge a fee upfront.

freebies

981 FREECYCLE IT

Freecycle is a global online network for people who want to swap items. Working on the premise that one person's trash is another's treasure, check out what they've got in your area or advertise to get rid of your stuff. See www.freecycle.org.

982 RECYCLE YOUR CANS

Did you know your local depot might actually pay you for taking your aluminium cans for recycling? Check out which depots offer incentives and store up your cans to take down there for a small but meaningful profit.

983 GO ON A TREASURE HUNT

Search your house and car for all that misplaced money – look in trouser and jacket pockets, 'safe' hiding places, old purses or bags, drawers, jewellery boxes, greetings and birthday cards, chair and sofa cushions and behind and under furniture. You'll be amazed how much you find.

984 JOIN A LIBRARY

Libraries are free (as long as you don't incur charges) and if you are a taxpayer you have in fact already paid for their services, so make the most of them. Investigate what your library offers and see how you can include it in your life to help you make savings.

985 SIGN ON

There are many websites offering you the chance to sign up for free samples, and the beauty is that once you've signed up with a manufacturer they will probably keep sending new product samples to you.

986 FREE READING

A good way of cutting the cost of a daily newspaper is to take advantage of any free papers being handed out at your train or underground (metro) station. Sometimes these are abbreviated versions of mainstream papers and other times more celebrity-based, but they usually carry the main headline stories.

987 BE A TESTER

Join the testing panel of your favourite magazine or local paper. Write to them explaining why you are a good choice (your lifestyle, appearance, job and so on) and they might include you in their consumer panels for free samples.

988 BOOK A SALE

Your local library will probably hold a book sale when they change their stock over. It might only be once a year but you can pick up some great bargains, and they even give some books away for free, so make sure you keep in contact with them to see when their sales might be.

989 ONLINE FREEBIES

For free clothing online (bear in mind that these will almost always be goods for publicity, like baseball caps, T-shirts and sweatshirts, but in some cases they are branded goods) visit www.coolfreebielinks.com, which carries a whole range of current bargains to be had internationally.

990 TEST FOR FREE

Write to the manufacturers of your favourite items (think beauty products, household cleaning products, and drink or food suppliers, to name but a few) and register to be on their testing panels. Or try the supermarkets for their own-brand products or specialist tester companies.

991 SELL OFF CHINA

If you have some old family china, particularly easily breakable items like teapots and jugs, think about approaching a specialist pottery sales company (there are many online). These companies will often pay good prices for single items as they specialize in tracking down the pieces people need to complete their sets.

992 GO AS A GROUP

If you book to visit an attraction as a group you can get a massive discount. Get a group of friends together to go with you and as long as you book in early you'll probably get a great deal.

993 TAKE A SURVEY

Often the best way to get free stuff is to take a survey, usually online. Just spend a few minutes filling in details and you will receive something free, such as samples, and usually an entry to a prize draw as well. Just make sure you tick the 'don't contact me' box unless you want to be inundated with extra e-mails.

994 CHOOSE START-UPS

New companies often offer free items to get customers through the door – T-shirt printers offer a free T-shirt, for instance, or get free lipsticks at cosmetics stores or free drinks at a new coffee shop.

995 BE IN THE AUDIENCE

You could be in the audience of your favourite TV show for free – contact the programme makers or check online to see when there are spaces and be prepared to go to midweek recordings to get a slot. Once there, see if they will do a backstage tour for free, as many TV companies offer them.

996 KNOW THE CODE

Visit one of the increasing number of online sites dedicated to sharing discount codes with the world and either print out vouchers or use the discount codes when buying online. However, do make sure you're entitled to use the discount, as some codes are only for the use of people who are actually sent them, so it's worth checking you're not doing anything illegal.

997 JOIN A PARENTING CLUB

Parenting clubs are a great way to get free samples and discounts on branded items for babies and kids. Join up to as many as you can and complete online surveys. Or register to be a tester for online parenting websites or clubs for even more free stuff.

998 GET FREE DEALS

There are loads of Internet companies all over the world listing free deals and how to get items for free. Usually they work by sending you a weekly e-mail of new offers so you can browse the deals to see if any work for you. Find them in your area by doing a search for 'get stuff for free'. Just make sure you're not seduced into buying something you don't need just because it's on offer.

999 APPROACH THE COMPANY

If there is a company whose products you buy regularly, approach them to see if you can get on their mailing list. There is usually a free customer-care line on packaging, and if you call them they will send you new products and special offers for free as they come out.

1000 TALKING FOR FREE

If you have a pay-as-you-go mobile phone (cell) you can get free minutes by doing online surveys (see www.phonelagoon.com). Alternatively ask friends for promo codes or join a free minutes network like Blyk that gives you free calls if you agree to receive a certain number of adverts a day. If you have a contract, always check with your provider, as they may offer monthly giveaway minutes and special offers.

1001 MARKET RESEARCH

Register on a market-research company website and they will send you e-mails letting you know the requirements – they will be looking for you to fit in with a certain customer profile, considering factors such as age, sex, marital status, children and products you use or the area in which you live. Usually it involves an hour or two of your time, pays well, and can take the form of a focus group, online survey, telephone interview, hall test, panel or face-to-face and telephone interviews.